MUSIC CAMP!

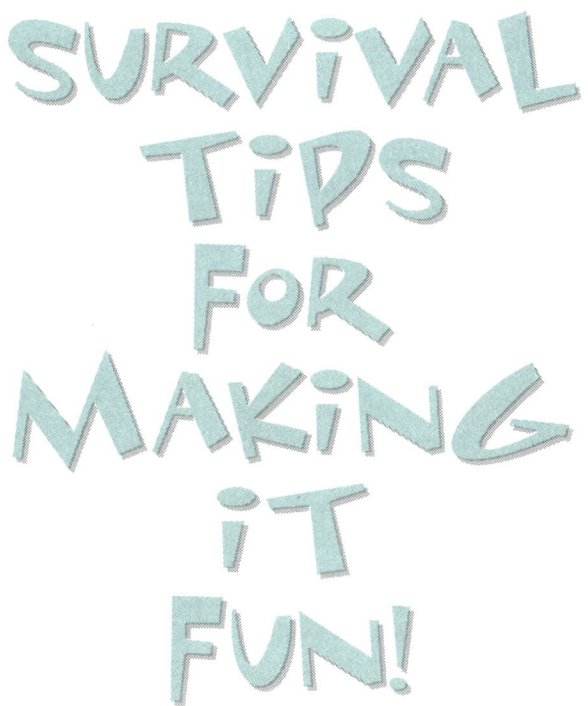

SURVIVAL TIPS FOR MAKING IT FUN!

Manual Written by Jeanne Bolin
Camp Developed by Don and Jeanne Bolin

CHURCH
STREET
PRESS

Church Street Press
Nashville, Tennessee

Dedication

As a pebble hits the water and the ripples unfold, a creative idea encourages more creativity.

*A special thank you to many innovative people who have contributed
special ideas from their unique fields of ministry.
It is our prayer for this project that the ripples in the water
will continue to reach outward and touch the lives of many children.*

*Thanks to Don Bolin and the Bolin Company—
Joseph, Benjamin, Joy, John, David, Daniel, and Faith.*

*Special Thanks to all staff and church families of:
Murdale Baptist Church, Carbondale, Illinois;
Lakeside Baptist Church, Canton, Texas;
Immanuel Baptist Church, Benton, Illinois;
as well as all the friends and staff of **Summer Week Of Choir**.
Sincere appreciation to Kathie Hill for her encouragement and counsel.*
— Jeanne Bolin

ISBN: 0633076309

Dewey Decimal Classification Number: 780.79
Subject Heading: MUSIC CAMPS\CAMPS\MUSIC—STUDY AND TEACHING

Printed in the United States of America

Music, Publishing, and Recording
LifeWay Church Resources
One LifeWay Plaza
Nashville, TN 37234-0160

Unless otherwise noted, Scripture quotations are taken from the *Holman Christian Standard Bible*,
© Copyright 2000 by Holman Bible Publishers. Used by permission.

Scripture quotations marked (NIV) are from the Holy Bible, *New International Version*,
© Copyright 1984, 1986 by Holman Bible Publishers. All rights reserved. Used by permission.

TABLE OF CONTENTS

chapter 5

PRODUCTION AND STAGING

chapter 6

Permission is granted to duplicate any part of Appendices A, B, and C.

Appendix A

Appendix B

Appendix C

Appendix D

chapter 1
GETTING STARTED

mission field, touching the lives of children, their parents, other family, and friends. It is our desire that you not only see the organization and details of a music camp, but that you will also catch the spirit of the week. We strongly believe, "Unless the Lord builds a house, its builders labor over it in vain; unless the Lord watches over a city, the watchmen stays alert in vain" (Psalm 127:1). We humbly ask for His blessings and pray that this work will not be in vain. We trust that it will plant a simple seed.

A Simple Seed

As a child, I attended a children's choir once a week at a local Baptist church. As we sang about the love of Jesus, I began to understand the story of salvation. The Lord spoke to my heart, and in childlike faith, I received His gift of forgiveness and salvation, and took hold of His work in my life. In years to come, my entire family would be affected by the ministry of this small children's choir.

That little Baptist church would never remember my name. They invested time and energy into my life with nothing in return except God's promise, in Isaiah, that His Word would not return empty. They just planted a simple seed.

Now, for over 25 years, my husband and I have worked in the music ministry. It has been our goal to be part of the seed planting business. We wanted to develop a music camp with three goals in mind:
1. Music emphasis
   •Children will learn and be part of a God-centered musical presentation.
2. Bible memory and character training
   •Children will learn Scripture verses and spiritual attributes.
3. Great fun and great activities
   •Provide a fun and active, yet Christ-centered, environment.

We look at music camp as a

What Is Music Camp?

For over 25 years, I have been aware of music camps and Summer Weeks Of Choir (SWOC) taking place all over the country. Music camp is a camp in which the emphasis is on singing and musical training. It is generally a ministry out of a church, staffed by church members, and designed to give children an opportunity to sing and perform on stage. The agenda combines different activities and classes to make for a fun, yet powerful, week. A children's musical or a collection of children's songs is presented at the end of the camp week. This culminating event is a time for sharing and celebration as well as worship and praise.

Even though music camps have been around for a long

OVERVIEW OF AN ALL-DAY 5-DAY CAMP

Monday or Day 1

8:00-8:30 a.m.	Staff Meeting with Coffee and Doughnuts
8:40-9:00 a.m	Early Bird Games
9:00-9:10 a.m.	Brief Opening Assembly
9:10-9:30 a.m.	Music Class 1
9:30-9:50 a.m	Music Class 2
9:50-10:10 a.m.	Music Class 3
10:10-10:30 a.m.	Music Class 4
10:30-10:50 a.m.	Bible study, activity class, or craft class
10:50-11:10 a.m.	Snacks/Recreation/ Bathroom Break
11:10-11:30 a.m.	Stage Class (placing children on stage)
11:40-12:15 p.m.	Mass Rehearsal
12:15-12:45p.m.	Lunch
12:45-1:05 p.m.	Music Class 5
1:05-1:25 p.m.	Music Class 6
1:25-1:45 p.m.	Bible study, activity class, or craft class
1:45-1:55	Bathroom Break
1:55-2:30	Mass Rehearsal
2:30-2:50	Snow Cones and Team Awards
2:50-3:05	Parents pick up Campers
3:30	Staff children picked up and child care closed

Tuesday or Day 2

Same as Day 1 until 11:10a.m.	
11:10-11:20a.m.	Bathroom Break
11:20-12:15 pm.	Mass Rehearsal
12:15-12:45 p.m.	Lunch
12:45-1:05	Music Class
1:05-1:25	Music Class
1:25-1:45	Bible study, activity class, or craft class
1:45-1:55	Bathroom Break
1:55-2:30	Mass Rehearsal
2:30-2:50	Snow Cones and Awards
2:50-3:05	Parents pick up campers
3:30	Staff children picked up and child care closed

Wednesday or Day 3

8:00-8:30 a.m.	Staff Meeting with Coffee and Doughnuts
8:40-9:00 a.m.	Early Bird Games
9:00-10:00 a.m.	Mass Rehearsal
10:00.-12:00p.m.	Carnival and Lunch
12:00-12:10p.m.	Bathroom Break
12:10 -12:30p.m.	Divide into groups; Pass out camp T-shirts
12:30-1:00 p.m.	Mass Rehearsal or Mass Activity/Class
1:00-1:30p.m.	Camp Picture taken
1:30-2:30 p.m.	Mass Rehearsal
2:30-2:50 p.m.	Snow Cones and Awards
2:50-3:05	Parents pick up campers
3:30	Staff children picked up and child care closed

Thursday or Day 4

8:00-8:30 a.m.	Staff Meeting with Coffee and Doughnuts
8:40-9:00a.m.	Early Bird Games
9:00-11:00a.m.	Mass Rehearsal
11:00-12:00 p.m.	Bible study, activity class, or craft class
12:00-12:30p.m.	Bathroom & Lunch
12:30-1:30 p.m.	Mass Rehearsal
1:30-2:30 p.m.	Mass Activity, or Recreation
2:30-2:50 p.m.	Snow Cones and Awards
2:50-3:05	Parents pick up campers
3:30	Staff children picked up and child care closed

Friday or Day 5

8:00-8:30 a.m.	Staff Meeting with Coffee and Doughnuts
8:40-9:00a.m.	Early Bird Games
9:00-11:00	Mass Rehearsal (Dress and technical)
11:00-11:15 a.m.	Bathroom Break (prepare for water games)
11:15-11:45 a.m.	Water games
11:45-12:00 p.m.	Snow Cones
12:00-12:30 p.m.	Early Dismissal

Friday Evening or "Opening Night"

6:00 -7:00 p.m.	Rehearsal, Individual pictures made on video
7:00 -8:00 pm.	Presentation of the musical

Sunday Evening or Second Presentation

6:00-7:00 p.m.	Rehearsal
7:00 -8:00 p.m.	Presentation followed by awards (Each group introduced and given certificates/camp pictures.)
8:00 p.m.	Reception

time, they are still a very well-kept secret to most music ministries. Music camp could be a new and fresh way of outreach to your community. It is our desire to give you detailed explanations of our camp procedures. We also want to show a broader picture of music camps and how they can be conducted in different church situations. We have consulted experienced people in the area of children's music camps to enhance our knowledge.

Whether you are considering a music camp ministry, wanting a new strategy for an existing music camp, or needing some fresh ideas for children's musical productions, it is our desire to show you the possibilities and the potential that await you.

Overview

It is said that a picture is worth a thousand words. If music camp is a new concept, we want to give you a basic overview of a camp. This is designed to give you an idea of how the different activities are put together to make a fun and meaningful, musical week. Page 6 shows a week at a glance. In the following chapters, however, we will discuss different options, schedules, classes, and special activities. You will decide what is best for your church and your individual camp. But first, take a look!

Camp Options and Considerations

We want to discuss many different ways and options for using a music camp program. At the same time, we would like to give various details about how our camp is designed. Kathie Hill calls it a "smorgasbord" of ideas. In other words, you have the opportunity to select from the many options what is best for your unique situation, or what appeals to you.

For years, our church had to have Vacation Bible School during the evening because almost every adult member worked outside the home during the day. In the last several years, that has changed. Now, we have a music camp during the day with more than enough leadership and staff, as well as a capacity enrollment of children. Every church has its own unique situations that will dictate when and how a camp can take place. Moreover, those decisions can even change from year to year.

Time Frames

Here are some different ways and different times to consider for your camp.
•Mon.–Fri. 9:00 am.–12:00 p.m. This is music camp with Vacation Bible School type hours. Your emphasis here would be primarily music, activities, and the production.
•Mon.–Fri. 9:00 a.m–3:00 p.m. This all-day camp is itemized in the overview with a mixture of music classes, mass rehearsals, recreation, snack/lunch, and other activities.
•Mon.–Fri. 9:00 a.m.–3:00 p.m. This all-day camp has classes and all rehearsals before lunch, followed by major camp activities in the afternoon. These activities could include swimming, bowling, skating, water park, horseback riding, miniature golf, a playland, or an amusement park.
•Mon.–Fri. 7:00 a.m.–5:30 p.m. This camp has extended hours to supply child care needs for parents who work.

•Mon.–Fri. 5:00/6:00 p.m.– 8:00 p.m. An evening camp where times may vary. Churches can feed the campers dinner to help working parents
•Sun.–Wed. 6:00 p.m–9:00 p.m. An evening camp Sunday, Monday, and Tuesday with the presentation of a short musical during a Wednesday night service.

When

Many music camps are held in the summer when children are out of school. But, why not

Some churches do not have a weekly children's choir program during the year. A music camp program in the summer could be a springboard to the development of a full time children's choir program.

consider a camp during spring break or a 3-day weekend? A mid-winter camp in February would add some warmth to a child's schedule. Start on a Thursday or Friday evening, work all day Saturday, and present the musical Saturday and Sunday evenings. Other camps are held the week before regular children's choir enrollment, as a "kick off" to the new year. We often schedule our camp the last full week of June and include the musical as a part of our annual church picnic, located at the city park, for the 4th of July celebration.

SURViVAL TiP

Be careful to plan a minimum of scenery, so scenery and props can be transported.

Whether it's the first week of August or the third week of July, it is nice to have an annual date on the calendar so parents can plan their summers to include this musical week. It is also a perfect time for grandparents to invite their grandchildren to come and visit for a week of great memories.

Some churches do not have a weekly children's choir program during the year. A music camp program in the summer could be a springboard to the development of a full-time children's choir program.

Who

Music camps can involve the children in different ways. Some churches have all age groups involved in camp. Depending on your activities, it might be wise to have only the older children, grades 4-6, attend music camp. Other camps are geared for children who have completed the first grade before they begin; therefore, the summer after their sixth grade year would be their final camp year.

We ask that children be six years old before September 1 to participate, and divide our camp into teams of children comprised of combined ages. It is nice to have the older campers mentor the younger children. This seems to defuse cliques and prevent attitude problems. In the activities we have chosen, the age-balanced teams compete well with each

other. Teams are able to stand on stage together because each team has many different heights. The combined age grouping also promotes great team spirit.

You may prefer that all of one grade level be together. Having children of the same age/grade in a team also has its benefits. For example, certain classes and activities are easier when the children are the same age. Some camps have the different age levels work on projects or costumes appropriate to their ages and exhibit them during the musical presentation.

How

Different denominations sometimes have neighboring churches that work together on a music camp. For example, one association of churches learned a Christmas musical during music camp. During the following Christmas season, each individual church presented that same musical for their own congregation, with their own children singing the solos and playing the lead roles. The congregations were thrilled because it was a way to bring children's music into the Christmas services, with far less pressure and preparation.

A certain Baptist church in Illinois had a music camp program for 10 years. Children would come from all over the state, as well as surrounding states, to be involved. The church even offered housing for children that wanted to participate. They went the extra mile in outreach to all children. They mailed letters to other Baptist churches in the state to advertise their camp.

Although this manual will give you a variety of ideas, it is your philosophy for the week that will give your music camp its form.

Some areas may have a city-wide children's choir. Why not take that basic idea and expand it to share the gospel? Meet once a week during the summer, either morning or evening; learn your musical the first month; then, sing every week until school starts. Double or triple cast all parts so there is no problem when someone leaves on vacation. You can do a concert or a children's musical in many different settings. Be careful to plan a minimum of scenery, so scenery and props can be transported. This same idea could also be expanded to an afternoon choir during the school year.

Why

So, you are looking for ministry? Why not choose an area in your city with special needs to have a music camp? An orphanage, a housing project, a community center, or a day care program are just a few

places that might be available. In our city, the state university has a large housing project for married students with families. There are so many children, and the staff is always looking for groups to come in and work with them. Our church has had block parties and backyard Bible clubs for the children. Why not have a music camp? Be sure to check the policies with any of these organizations concerning Christian music and the use of Scripture.

Is your church planning a mission trip? Why not plan a children's musical as part of your program? It is a perfect way to get the parents out for an evening service. If the program is presented outdoors, practice alone can be a great advertisement!

SURVIVAL TIP

Double or triple cast all parts so there is no problem when someone leaves on vacation.

Why not consider adding a musical to your Vacation Bible School program? Some churches could not support two major weeks such as VBS and a music camp. Combining them could be a solution.

Remember this—a large children's choir is wonderful, but it is not essential. A small, enthusiastic ensemble of children can be just as impressive. Big smiles, wholehearted singing, and simple outfits will win many a heart, whether you have 10, 25, or 100 singers.

Obviously, there are many other possibilities. Evaluate your situation and ask the Lord to impart a vision for your church and community. Experience the ministry and the fun of music camp.

> It is the director's job to plan a camp that has great purpose...

Evaluate Where You Are

The following considerations will help you determine some expectations and limitations:

- Will the church support this ministry through prayer, involvement, and financial necessity?
- What is the enrollment of the church?
- What is the children's Sunday School attendance, and how many children from the church can be expected to enroll?
- What is Vacation Bible School enrollment?
- How many workers can be expected to volunteer?
- Financially, will this be self-sustaining, or will the church have to help support this ministry?
- Are there other churches in the area doing music camps? In our community, there is a Vacation Bible School taking place almost every week of the summer. We are the only church that has a music camp; therefore, we have children attend from churches all over the region.
- Are there any special needs or situations that should be considered before taking on this project? (e.g. Will we need to rent extra sound and lighting equipment? Do we have the necessary space for activities, classes, and the performance(s)?)

Primary Purpose and Mission Statement

The thought of planning a whole week of music camp can be very overwhelming. I have found that planning is really an extension of myself. The concepts and principles that are important for me to build within my home and children are the blocks with which I build when planning music camp. It is important to analyze your purpose for the camp. What are your unique gifts? What is your message? What do the children of your church and/or community need? As the mother of seven children who has home educated them for 15 years, I bring many of those home-schooling ideas and goals to the camp planning table. I am also grateful to my staff who brings gifts and insights that give our camp variety and balance.

Some directors may have a goal to develop basic skills in music theory. Others may emphasize evangelism. Some churches have people who are gifted in crafts, and no day is complete without a special craft creation. Some directors may sense a real need to reach out to the community and build good public relations. Others may want to plan a camp as an encouragement to smaller churches with little or no music programs. Many people are gifted teachers, and planning a time of Bible activities and study is a must. The musical itself may dictate an emphasis, whether it is evangelism, Christian example, or making a stand for what is right. Will your ministry be to children that like to sing? It is a different ball game in a music camp when you are dealing with children that like to sing, rather than a music camp with children who are tolerating the music until recreation.

We come to this table of preparation from different directions. It is the director's job to plan a camp that has great purpose rather than just filling in the time periods. So, as you march ahead, be encouraged. Get excited! Your adventure has only just begun.

It's Time to Talk Green

Budget Issues

My very least favorite topic concerning music camp is money. The "green stuff" is necessary, though, to accomplish some of the special things desired during this week. It may not take as much money as one might think. A wise person counts the cost before jumping into a project. Let us be wise; then, and do a little counting!

It is very possible to stage a children's musical fairly inexpensively. An accompaniment track ($80.00), several rehearsal recordings ($50.00) and singer's scores($25.00), the Leader's Guide/Teacher's Manual ($50.00), and, of course, this book will all provide a good foundation and give a sense of direction. If your camp is small, it will take less material. The larger your camp, the greater the need for more music and materials.

Registration Fees

Registration fees are a way to absorb some of the cost. They can range from $10.00 to $50.00 or more. If major day camp activities are included,

such as a water park, an amusement park, or other activities away from church, this fee could be even higher.

Sometimes there is a family limit to the fees. For example, $25.00 per child or $60.00 per family, regardless of the number of children. Some camps allow a $35.00 fee for the first child, with a $20.00 fee for other children in the family. It is good to think through what the total incoming fees will be. Our registration fee is $50.00 per child. With 100 children enrolled, our budget is approximately $5,000. We make no allowances for families who have several children, nor do we give a free scholarship to a child whose parent is on the camp staff. However, we do offer a scholarship to any child that is truly in need. We have established a *Send-a-Kid-to-Camp* campaign to help raise money for these expenses.

With the registration money, the camp provides a listening recording and student book of the musical; a camp T-shirt; a camp picture; a full week of snacks; and a carnival with prizes, activities, and games. In addition, we purchase equipment; build special staging; provide T-shirts, breakfast, and a nice retreat room for the staff; present a full production with all the trimmings; and host a closing fellowship for all camp families. We do not

SURVIVAL TIP

Offer a scholarship to any child that is truly in need. Establish a *Send-a-Kid-to-Camp* campaign to help raise money for these expenses.

apologize for the registration fee because we turn around and invest every dime back into the camp week. Also, we have $500.00 in the church budget as a cushion for unexpected expenses.

Scholarships
Send-a-Kid-to-Camp
The cost to each camper is $50.00, which includes one lunch (during our carnival), T-shirt, recording and book (one per family), camp picture, refreshments, and a week of wonderful activities. This can be a financial hardship for some families. We do not advertise that we offer scholarships. Two weeks before camp begins, however, we set up a table in the church foyer displaying forms and asking people to provide music camp scholarships for needy children. (See Form PE-7 in Appendix A.) We offer full scholarships of $50.00 and half-scholarships of $25.00. We try to address this discreetly when a need is discovered. God has always provided the funds to take care of our scholarship needs.

Staff Discounts
In some church music camps, you are entitled to one free registration for your child or grandchild if you are on the camp staff. If we did this at our church, we would have at least 25 scholarships given to our staff ($1,250.00). At this point, the camp cannot run financially without this money. However, if there is a staff person whose child needs a scholarship, that child is given priority.

With so many visitors—family and friends of these children—and because of our $50.00 registration fee, we do not charge admission or take an offering during the musical presentations. Some camps do, and it helps defray the costs. We have struggled with this decision of an offering, money that might help to pay for staff scholarships. We have chosen, instead, for the week to be a time to lovingly reach out to these families, not asking them for anything more than an opportunity to minister to them and their children.

Some camps give a discount for the second and third child. We made a decision with furnishing the book, the tape, and all the extras, that parents are getting a great deal for their $50.00. We do not apologize for this registration fee. After seeing all that we do in a week, the fee is rarely questioned. Sometimes people pay installments of $10.00 per week, but we ask that it be completely paid by the first day of camp.

One night during the presentation, I make sure the teachers come stand at the front. I introduce them, and explain to the audience that these work-

ers have invested 40-50 hours of service in the week and have also paid for their own children to attend. What a team of workers we have!

Cutting Costs/ Budget Busters
It is not necessary to have a registration fee. My first music camp, over 20 years ago, was set up like a Vacation Bible School. We simply expanded our basic Sunday evening children's choir program. Our activities, Bible stories, theory, and learning of the songs all took place in the regular children's graded choir class with the same teachers that usually taught on Sunday night. Then, we would move to the auditorium and work together as a mass group on the musical. There was no carnival or any other extra activities. We did not build an expensive stage or backdrop. Everything was very simple. The musical we chose combined an adult soloist with the children's songs. We invited a special guest to perform the solos. This created an extra expense for the week, but we learned that the people were so interested in the children that it became obvious our special guest was not the highlight of the evening. The children were! AMEN! We repeated the musical later with an adult church member

singing the solo part.
The production expenses for your musical can also be kept to a minimum. Sometimes church members will donate items or volunteer their time to help build and work on constructing a stage set. A supportive team of parents can be one of the best resources. Many times, parents are just waiting for someone to ask them to help solve a problem or provide an answer. (See Form ST-2 in Appendix A.) Business people in your church or your

community might donate T-shirts with their business name on the back for an advertisement in your program. A simple pair of jeans, khakis, or shorts with a solid-color T-shirt can become an inexpensive costume. Most communities have a thrift shop. With a little imagination, you could create just about anything you need. Have the children design and make their own costumes. Ask a church member to make a video of the musical instead of hiring a professional. You can cut many corners to make it work.

Staging can be very simple and inexpensive. Let the children design and create your backdrop. Special lighting and extra sound are great, but they are not absolutely necessary. There are wonderful accounts of great men of God who preached to thousands of people without having even a microphone. In fact, Jesus did that same thing many times, and it never affected his presentation!

Some churches take an offering at the close of each performance. That is another way to cover expenses and can involve more people in the giving process.

This allows grandparents, friends, and other guests an opportunity to be a part of the week. Be aware, though, when parents have paid a substantial registration fee, they may not appreciate being asked to give an offering.

You can survive without listening tapes or CDs and books. It is just easier for us to let that be part of the registration fee. If you choose not to have a fee, the parents can purchase them. When our adult choir begins a musical, the church buys the listening tapes in bulk, and the choir members can then

SURVIVAL TIP

With a little imagination, you could create just about anything you need. Have the children design and make their own costumes.

purchase them at a discounted price. This idea will work if you offer a listening tape/CD for parents to purchase for their campers. That would also help defray expense.

Other camp costs can be modified to be less expensive as well. Choose activities that are cost free. A visit from the fire department is a great activity and is usually free. In the summer, water games are always a hit! Children love to play all types of games. This is another inexpensive way to add a lot of fun with no cost. As your camp grows, you can add more expensive activities along the way.

Do not serve refreshments twice a day, and/or delete the Sunday night fellowship. Providing camp shirts for your staff is a wonderful gesture, but you would rather have a music camp than T-shirts. Look for any way to save money, yet still remain true to your vision for ministry.

Finance is an issue unique to each church. Some programs are completely supported by the church budget. Some churches have opened a separate music camp account at the bank to keep their funds totally separate and available to the music camp leadership. Other churches would have a problem with that concept. Finance is a process determined by priorities; therefore, it is important to have an understanding with your pas-

1997 Summer Week Of Choir Income & Expenses

Income

$3,860.00	Registration Fees
$691.00	Scholarships
$875.00	Videos/T-shirts
Total Income $5,426.00	

Expenses

$100.00	Petty Cash Purchases
$112.33	Mailing-Tapes & Books
$4.78	Mailing
$50.00	Refund of Registration Fee
$50.00	Petty Cash Purchases
$65.81	Supplies
$100.00	Bounce Around
$176.05	Photographs
$150.00	Childcare
$20.00	Childcare
$500.00	Soundcore-Sound & Lighting
$65.00	Supplies
$50.00	Quiz-Off Video & Manual
$42.28	Lumber
$675.46	Music Books & Tapes
$1,129.50	Nic at Night T-Shirts
$8.00	Postcards
$53.78	Supplies
$108.00	Advertising
$110.00	Certificates
$200.04	Prizes
$23.00	Supplies
$15.95	Stationery
$875.00	Nic at Night Videos
$100.00	Quiz-Off Medals
$151.05	Nic at Night T-Shirts
$375.21	Fellowship
$43.02	Supplies
$46.49	Supplies
$173.27	Cups/Supplies
$11.96	Supplies
$22.70	Batteries
$8.41	Supplies
Total Expenses $5,617.09	

Total Income	$5,426.00
- Total Expenses	$5,617.09
	($191.09)

tor and finance committee about how to deal with this issue. We must be accountable for our spending, but we also need the freedom to make the camp run smoothly.

Do not let the color green discourage you. People want to see their children sing, perform, and share the message of Christ. You may have to do without some things the first year. You may not have all that you would like to have after four, five, or even 10 years. The Lord has promised to supply every need, not every

desire. When people see the children and get excited about what they are doing, your resources will begin to grow. You will also learn to be very creative with what you have. (See Form PE-1 in Appendix A for budget planning form examples.)

chapter 2

PROMOTION AND ENROLLMENT

Advertisement and Publicity

T-shirts

Look at catalogs and begin the process of selecting T-shirts. See what is available through the music publishers of your selected musical. Also, investigate companies in your area that create and produce clothing for advertising purposes. Discuss with a representative your needs and financial concerns or limitations. Alert them to the camp dates and when you would need to acquire the shirts.

T-shirts have several purposes. They create unity and team spirit. They will promote and advertise music camp and your church all year long. T-shirts can also be worn as the basic costume for the presentation of the musical.

Join the FUN at Music Camp!

Many factors influence the cost of T-shirts:
- printing on the front only, versus front and back
- using one or more colors For example, if three colors are used, the shirts must go through the printing process three times. Each color adds to the cost.
- the quality of the material
- the quantity purchased

There are different ways to order T-shirts.

Publisher's T-shirts

Some music publishing companies design their own T-shirts emphasizing a specific musical.

The shirts are already designed to have a lot of personality and there are no difficult design or layout decisions to be made. Moreover, there are no copyright issues to be investigated, made, or fees to be paid. This can alleviate many problems.

Timing the delivery of the shirts will take some preparation. If you are unsure of the number of each size to order, ask how early an order needs to be placed so that it is processed in time. In addition, ask how quickly extra shirts can be shipped and what the return policy is on shirts that are not used.

Custom-Designed T-shirts

A local screen printing company can provide the opportunity to design your own shirt. This option also takes some preparation. Be sure to start this process early. If you want to use art from your musical, permission must be granted by, and fees paid to, the music publisher.

We enjoy designing our own, T-shirts. We determine the message on the T-shirt and can personalize the back of the shirts with the church name and camp dates. Remember, however, the design and its message should be of the highest quality and reflect the image your church wishes to convey.

Color

Another T-shirt consideration is color. Colors can also be determined by the musical. I always keep my eyes open for how other performances use color. One show had four colors that I would have never put together; yet, it was dynamic on stage. Color is a wonderful tool to enhance the stage. Obviously, this is another choice that depends on preference.

Darker, bolder colors are preferable over pastels. Lighter colors seem to wash out under stage lights, while bolder colors add more personality. T-shirts can be purchased that already have unique designs and colors on them. The cost of these special T-shirts is often the same as solid-colored ones. When choosing a shirt to be worn for the presentation, choose a simple, focused logo. Strive for a unified, precise message. Emphasize the faces of the children rather than characters on the shirts. Another bit of advice, be sure to look for differences in shirt quality. All material is not the same. Take into consideration the fabric content and weight when making decisions.

Sizes and Quantities

Ask the shirt company for several sizes of the T-shirts to display during registration. T-shirt sizes can vary, and many parents will want to look at a sample before ordering. Toward the end of registration, inform the shirt company of the sizes and quantities needed for the children and staff along with an estimate of possible extra shirts. It is good to allow 8-10 days for shipping. After your first camp, take the order from the previous year as a starting point, ordering more as needed. It is always better to have a few extras than not enough. Extras can be sold at the musical presentations or given away; this is good publicity for your church and children's music program. Be careful when ordering small sizes. We never order a small child T-shirt for a camper. Those shirts are quite small. It is safer to go with a larger size than one that might be too little.

There is a place on the camp registration form (Form PE-3) for parents to order extra shirts for their families. The money for these shirts should be included with the registration checks. Based on a camp enrollment of 100, we order 200 T-shirts (100 for the campers, 10–15 for staff children in child care, 30–40 for camp and church staff, plus 25–50 extra). We sell the T-shirts to the parents and our church members for a slightly inflated price. This provides a little extra cash and helps pay for any shirts not sold.

We distribute the T-shirts on Wednesday of camp just before the photographer comes and takes a camp picture. We do this so that everyone has a clean camp T-shirt for the picture. This also allows everyone to get his or her shirt at the same time—there's always so much excitement!

As you recruit workers for your music camp, be sure to get a T-shirt size from them. If the shirts are ordered and arrive early enough, the leaders could have them to wear on Monday morning. This will add so much excitement as well as help parents and campers recognize the staff.

We can "bear-ly" wait until Music Camp starts!

Teaser

Once or twice before the camp week begins, arrange for a "teaser." A teaser is designed to be a quick advertisement

with a musical idea or theme that will create interest and excitement about the camp musical. This is best done during a Sunday morning service. It can be any of the following:
- short song
- a few funny lines from a song or scene in the musical
- walk in wearing a unique costume
- short skit or part of a scene
- a conversation with two staff workers
- a child praying for the week
- Early Bird song that the children can sing
- A simple hat, hand prop, or background music can set a funny or very serious mood.

Regular announcements are made all the time. Spice them up! Have some fun. Do something that people will remember and that will get their attention. A teaser is a red flag that says, "I want you to know about Music Camp, and we want you to come see our presentation. We want you to enroll your children!"

Enrollment

Prospects
Especially for the first year, prepare a mailing list of prospective campers. This list can come from many sources:
- the children's Sunday School enrollment
- public schools, area Christian and other private schools
We have a Christian school that meets at our church, but

they would not give us a list of names and addresses. They did agree to hand out a publicity sheet about the camp to each student.
- churches in your particular denominational association
- other local churches
- local clubs—Awanas, Girl Scouts®, etc.
- previous campers

You can also advertise in the local newspapers as well as radio and television stations. (Many have a free Community Calendar segment.)

Initial Mailing
The advertisement/ prospect mailing needs to be sent six to eight weeks before your camp dates. If you are sending a packet to a church, be sure and tell them to make as many copies as they need. You should have plenty of copies of the registration forms available for the people who call the office and want one mailed to them or for people who will come and pick some up at the church office. We have now reached a point, after four years, that we do not need to advertise in the paper or mail to local churches. Our former campers and parents are the best advertisements we have. This prosepctive camper mailing should contain the following:
❏ standard form letter which describes the camp

❏ registration form (campers can mail it back to the church or bring by personally)
❏ audition information form (See Forms PE-2, PE-3, and PS-1 in Appendix A.)

Receiving Registration Forms and Checks
We encourage campers to get their registration forms in quickly. Every church will process these forms differently, but usually the Camp Registration Director/Camp Secretary or church secretary handles this task. As the forms are received, the information is entered into a computer database. Also, the date that the form is received and the check number are recorded on the form. All checks are given to the Finance Director after the forms have been processed.

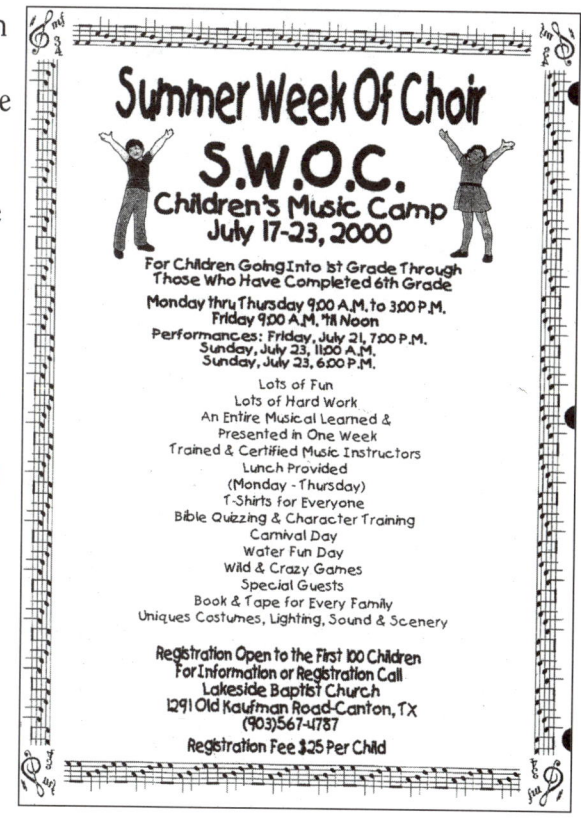

One advantage to having the same teams every year is that it cuts down on a great deal of preparation. Once the basic posters and organizational materials are made, they are ready for use year after year.

For several years, we made the statement on the registration forms that we could only enroll 100 children. This idea came from another church in our state that had a music camp ministry for years, and we never questioned it. Last year, our registration letters were mailed and eight days later, we had enrolled over 100 children. We started our waiting list but determined that our building had adequate space for more campers. We changed our policy. The Lord blessed us with plenty of staff; and, with a few changes, we managed the extra children. Our stage would need some modifications, but there were men in our church who quickly volunteered to tackle the job. Our only true concern was adequate space for the audience during the presentations. We would be pushing our fire code limit. The solution was to give two performances each night and divide the crowd in half. It worked!

I share this story to emphasize how important it is to consider policies. Again, what is right and works for one church could be a hindrance to another. This should serve as as a reminder to always evaluate your own situation.

Scholarships

The Camp Registration Director, Camp Secretary, or whoever is in charge of processing camper registrations, must be made aware of any scholarships or available fee reductions. If the recipients of these are known, that information should be provided as well. (See p. 11-12 for descriptions of these discounts.)

Assigning the Campers to Groups

A tool of our camp's organization is assigning the campers into teams or groups. The group names are as follows:

Blue Bobcats (BB)
Green Giraffes (GG)
Orange Orangutans (OO)
Purple Pandas (PP)
Red Rhinos (RR)
Yellow Yaks (YY)

These team names are only suggestions. You may want to use names that carry out the theme of your musical. One advantage to having the same teams every year is that it cuts down on a great deal of preparation. Once the basic posters and organizational materials are made, they are ready for use year after year.

An adult group leader and a youth group leader are assigned to every group. When we had our first camp with an enrollment of 60, we only had four groups (15 per group). The next year with 100 campers, we increased to six groups. With 138 campers, we used eight groups and put 17-18 children in a group. If you have a larger camp, 15-20 children per group is a maximum. It is also a good idea to keep the groups and members to even numbers when possible. Divide the groups so that each group has an equal mix of younger and older children. An older child can mentor a younger child, which demands character from the older campers toward the younger ones.

On the Registration Form, there is a place for any **special instructions**. Sometimes, brothers and sisters need to be together; sometimes they need to be separated. Friends are the same way. We allow parents to make those requests and, if at all possible, we work it out. One parent wrote that her daughter had been a Yellow Yak for three years and asked if she could be a Blue Bear. It is difficult because there are many considerations, and we may not know the child or the special situation. If in the first day you notice a problem in a group, do not hesitate to make changes.

Also, you want the children to make new friends. One year, we were asked to put a little girl in a group with a friend. We gladly made that adjustment. After all the groups had been set, the same parent called back again and asked if we would change two more girls and put them in her daughter's group. Then another parent called the Tuesday of camp and explained that another little friend wanted to be in that same group with all

her friends; and, she would not come back unless she was changed. All of a sudden, we were way out of bounds. It was truly not the best for the girls or their team. Consider your policies very carefully. Unless there is a very good reason for a special request, I suggest no changes once the groups have been assigned.

Nitty-Gritty Division
Using the information that has been entered into the database from registration, sort the campers by age. If you need to make any special assignments from parents' requests, flag those children's names so you can be sure they are in the right place later in the process. While the campers are in this sorted order by ages, assign the first six-year-old child to Blue Bears, the second six-year-old child to Green Giraffes, and the third to the Orange Orangutans, and on down the list of six-year-olds. Then, repeat the process with the seven-year-olds, followed by the eight-year-olds, etc. Remember, to go back to the Blue Bears every seventh child. Each group should have an evenly divided team by age. After entering this information into the database, you can now sort the list based on the team name. This will show who is on each team and allow any adjustments to be made. Check to see that parents' special requests (i.e. flagged names) have been honored as your policies allow.

SURVIVAL TIP

Every decision concerning music camp should always be made through prayer and God's direction.

Looking at each team, you will be able to see if they are relatively balanced according to age group. Teams will need to be assigned before the final mailing. Remember, however, that registration forms will still be coming in, even up through the Monday and Tuesday of camp week. When a late registration form does come in, check the age of the child, find a group needing that age child, and assign him or her to that group. If you have a group that contains 17 children and a group that has 15, you may want to add the child to the smaller group, even though that team may not need a child that age. It is important to try to balance the groups by age, yet still keep all close to the same total number of children.

Keep a list current of each group and the number of children per age. Once camp has begun, changes may be necessary to obtain a better balance between personalities, ages, and energy levels. Be of good courage. We seldom have had to change any child. We experienced very few problems in this area. To Him, we give the credit and the praise! Every decision concerning music camp, even these details, should always be made through prayer and God's direction.

Group Signs and Designations

There are illustrations for each of the team animals in

Appendix B. Enlarge the picture and attach it to poster board. (The art could be taken to a copy center or office supply store for professional enlargement.) Make two posters for each animal. Color or paint the animals. Place the colored posters back to back and laminate together so the same animal shows on each side. Cut a small opening at the bottom center of the laminated posters for a dowel rod to be inserted between them. Use a piece of strong tape around the base of the poster to hold the dowel rod in place. Additional smaller signs can be made for the registration tables at this time as well.

Our church has large orange traffic cones that are used in the parking lot during overcrowded Sundays. We use these cones, and the large posters with dowel rods placed inside, to set in the aisles of the auditorium so children will know where their group is sitting when they arrive. After the opening assembly, we move cones and posters to the fellowship hall, setting them at the end of the tables to designate where each team will sit for lunch. Any time there is a need to divide kids quickly into groups, a group leader can raise the team poster, and children will move immediately to that spot. On Sunday night, when each individual team is recognized after the musical presentation, it is nice to bring the posters up on stage and let the children hold them.

SURVIVAL TIP

It is important to try to balance the groups by age, yet still keep all close to the same total number of children.

Final Mailing Packet

Before the final packet can be mailed, you must have

❏ student books of the musical & listening tapes/CDs (one book and one recording per family)

❏ a letter that gives the final details for camp (See Form PE-6 in Appendix A.) Each registered camper should be assigned to a color-coded group by now. In this letter, tell the campers the name of their group, and stick a colored circle to the letter to help them remember. Each camper in a family will receive a separate letter. For example, if a family has three children, each child will receive a letter with his or her name on it indicating the assigned color-coded group. To save on mailing costs, all three letters should be placed in the same packet with the one music book and recording for the family.

❏ an audition response (acceptance/encouragement) letter for each child who auditioned (See Forms PS-3 and PS-4 in Appendix A.) On the acceptance letter, there is a place for the page number of the solo or speaking part. Include a phone number so parents can call if they have any questions.

This packet needs to be mailed about two weeks before camp begins, so that the children can begin memorizing their parts.

Registration

After Tuesday of camp week, we do not register any new children. The registration staff (two or three people) still needs to greet children every morning to ensure that the children get their lunches in the proper color-coded team bucket and have their name tags properly displayed.

We set the registration area outside the front of the building. Your registration area needs to be a place that is highly visible, easily accessible, and very spacious. Have a set of tables labeled with team names for campers who have already registered and another table for new registrants. There should be several workers per table. One person should be assigned the responsibility of welcoming and directing all campers to their assigned team's table.

Campers Already Registered

In the final mailing, all pre-registered campers are already assigned to a color coded team (Blue Bears, Yellow Yaks, Red Rhinos, etc.). The letter instructs children to look for their color/animal at registration. Upon arrival, the children will find a table that has their team animal and color. These need to be clearly marked. The children will check in, receive their color-coded name tag, and place their lunch in a color-coded team bucket. The children then proceed to the Opening Assembly area where Early Bird activities are already in progress.

We do not encourage parents to linger. If a parent is uneasy and would like to see what is happening, welcome them to sit near the back and observe for a few minutes. It is best for parents not to follow their children to their classes.

At the tables for campers already registered, include:
- color-coded name tags in alphabetical order, according to teams
- color-coded dots in case of changes
- master registration list
- blank name tags and a felt-tip marker
- note paper for any special instructions from parents

New Camper Registration

If a child has not registered, direct parents to the New Registration table to fill out a registration form. Be sure any new registrants' forms and fees are given to the Registration Director or Camp Secretary to enter this information into the computer database. An updated list of teams and members should be

> Your registration area needs to be a place that is highly visible and easily accessible ...

given out Tuesday morning during the 8:00 a.m. staff meeting.

At the New Registration table, include
- chairs where parents can sit to fill out forms
- clipboards with registration forms
- pens
- blank name tags
- money box
- note paper for any special instructions from parents
- color-coded dots
- listening tapes/CDs and students books (one per family)
- all correspondence previously mailed out, minus the audition information form

Assign the new campers to teams, determined by which team needs a child of that age, and give them temporary nametags.

Next, put color-coded dots on their lunches and place them in the corresponding color-coded team buckets. The children are then ready to enter and join the Early Bird activities.

Special Registration Instructions
Lunches
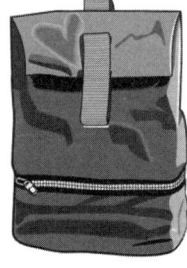
Some parents ask that their child's lunch be refrigerated.
If serving lunch, determine a policy and include instructions about lunches in the registered

camper mailing. Suggest sending a cold pack with the lunch. You may also want to remind parents of this in a daily newsletter if you print one.

Guidelines for Medication and Illness
Develop clear policies concerning a sick child or a child that consistently feels bad. We prefer not to give out medication, but a camp nurse could be available to discuss any unique problems regarding a child and medication. A permission slip with exact information should be filled out and signed by the parent when necessary. Have an emergency phone number where a caregiver can be reached anytime, any day of camp.

Dismissal Time
Name tags will be collected by the group leaders during the closing session. Group leaders pass out any lunch boxes. Name tags should be alphabetized and ready for the next 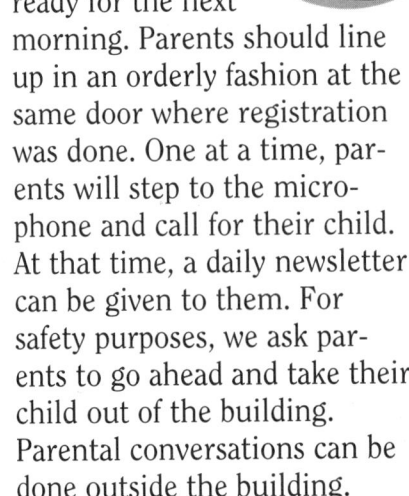 morning. Parents should line up in an orderly fashion at the same door where registration was done. One at a time, parents will step to the microphone and call for their child. At that time, a daily newsletter can be given to them. For safety purposes, we ask parents to go ahead and take their child out of the building. Parental conversations can be done outside the building.

This helps to identify any child who is still waiting for a parent or adult.

Safety Precautions
- Be alert that no child slips out of the building without a parent (danger: unattended children in a busy parking lot).
- Double check that name tags are removed before children leave the building.
- If a parent alerts a staff member that their child could be in danger due to an unauthorized parent or person trying to pick them up, all staff should be alerted. The Registration Director and the Group Leader should be especially cautious.

chapter 3
PLANNING THE SCHEDULE*

*It is best to read through this chapter, as well as the entire manual, one time before you begin to plan your schedule.

At that point, you will have read about different options, classes, activities, and special events, and will be better prepared to make scheduling decisions. Return to this section; then, and answer the necessary questions to begin penciling in your plans. Just remember this phrase as you plan—"One step at a time."

Securing Dates

These are brief descriptions of some major activities or items that you might need to secure dates for early in the planning process. As you progress through the manual, more detailed explanations will be given for various activities. It's your call whether to include these areas in your camp.

Music Camp Week
Get this on the calendar! We have found that the last full week of June is the best time for our church. Toward the end of the summer, vacation plans seem to be more of a conflict in our area. It has also been very strategic to have our music camp at the same time every year. This allows parents to plan their vacation around camp week. This may sound a bit arrogant, but if you produce a quality musical camp and program, parents will be happy to plan their calendars accordingly. Another reason we schedule our music camp for the last week of June is that it falls close to July 4th. Each year, our church celebrates at a local park as a community outreach tool.

Incorporating a portion of the musical into this event is an additional way of presenting the gospel to our community. Moreover, it brings the camp families back together again in a very relaxed atmosphere which provides just another opportunity to visit and fellowship with them.

Check to make sure that your Vacation Bible School and other programs on the church calendar do not conflict with music camp. Plenty of time should be allowed between any major church-wide activities. Often, you will find that the volunteers for music camp staff also work in VBS; therefore, they need time to rest. Make sure that there are no weddings or special activities on the weekend prior to, or following, music camp. You will need access to the entire facility during this time. In addition, set the dates for your cast auditions and any extra rehearsals. These should be placed on the church calendar as well.

Once all dates have been cleared, you are free to begin scheduling other activities or items such as: ordering costumes and T-shirts, sound equipment and lighting, prizes or craft items, and any special guests or features. A checklist has been provided to assist you with these details.

Special Events and Guests

If you are asking special guests to come speak at your camp, make sure you schedule those dates early. A special guest can capture the attention of the children and reinforce the camp message. Look for people in your area that have a unique talent or testimony. For example, during "The Secret of My Success," we looked for Christians who displayed "success" in character and in their daily lives. We invited an Olympic high jumper to share how his faith made a difference in striving for the gold medal. A local ventriloquist joined us another year to help with Bible stories and character lessons. She and her little friend even made a special appearance during the musical presentation.

Other special guests can spice up your week. Here are a few suggestions:

- Invite a juggler, clown, or mime to entertain.
- Rent a costume of a specific animal for a volunteer to wear.
- Dress up as a character from the Bible or from history.
- puppets
- skits
- Christian police officer, firefighter, or other public official
- a local or volunteer fire department

Our Senior Adults have a band with many unique instruments. The children enjoy hearing and playing some of these interesting instruments.

MUSIC CAMP PLANNING CHECKLIST

6 Months to 1 Year before Camp

- ☐ Pray for wisdom.
- ☐ Select a date for camp and put on church calendar.
- ☐ Set dates for auditions and extra rehearsals; put on church calendar.
- ☐ Invite/book any special guests.
- ☐ Choose a musical.
- ☐ Begin to advertise and publicize.
- ☐ Begin recruiting staff.

4-6 Months before Camp

- ☐ Pray for guidance.
- ☐ Intensify staff recruitment.
- ☐ Order music books and recordings.
- ☐ Begin ordering costumes or order materials and begin preparations for making costumes.
- ☐ Decide to order T-shirts and order samples.
- ☐ Reserve food and game machines for carnival.
- ☐ Rent sound and lighting equipment.
- ☐ Order quizzing equipment.
- ☐ Intensify publicity.
- ☐ Secure photographer and videographer.

3 Months before Camp

- ☐ Pray for direction.
- ☐ Develop classes.
- ☐ Create prospective camper mailing list.
- ☐ Order carnival prizes.
- ☐ Complete recruitment of staff.
- ☐ Continue to promote, publicize, and advertise the camp.

6-8 Weeks before Camp

- ☐ Pray and read the Bible daily.
- ☐ Mail prospective camper registration packet.
- ☐ Staff list should be almost complete.

4 Weeks before Camp

- ☐ Pray and read a Psalm daily.
- ☐ Finalize staff assignments.
- ☐ Confirm schedule and make copies for staff meeting.
- ☐ Plan first staff meeting.
- ☐ Begin assigning campers to groups.
- ☐ Hold cast auditions.
- ☐ Continue to promote, publicize, and advertise music camp.

2 Weeks before Camp

- ☐ Pray for patience and for the camp staff.
- ☐ Mail final packet to registered campers. (These campers should already be assigned to teams.)
- ☐ Cast assignments should be made by now.
- ☐ Have the first staff meeting.
- ☐ All costumes must be ordered or made by now.
- ☐ Begin to build stage and prepare set design.
- ☐ Begin scholarship campaign.
- ☐ Order all T-shirts.

1 Week before Camp

- ☐ Pray and read a Proverb daily.
- ☐ Meet with Kitchen Coordinator and Carnival Coordinator regarding food.
- ☐ Check with Sunday Night Reception Coordinator regarding plans for the reception and food.

2-3 Days before Camp

- ☐ Pray and read Matthew 5:1-16.
- ☐ Basic staging should be in place.
- ☐ First cast rehearsal—work with all soloists; block scenes with speakers/actors.
- ☐ Develop Bible quiz questions.
- ☐ Look at enrollment and make preliminary stage chart.
- ☐ Read Final Preparations section at the end of this chapter.

The Camp Agenda

Okay! Okay! I know that scheduling can be a real pain! If you looked at 10 school or camp schedules from across the country, you would probably find many different approaches to scheduling. So many factors can come into play. As we think of a "smorgasbord" idea, the questions in this chapter will help you start selecting activities and classes to individualize your music camp.

It would be wise to calculate the total number of minutes for one day. If you are planning a three-hour camp, for example, there would be 180 minutes per day. Our six-hour camp, plus 20 minutes for Early Bird games, means we have 380 minutes per day. Use one of the sample schedules and pencil in the classes that interest you. Make sure to have a good eraser as you work through the schedule! Blank scheduling forms (SC-1, SC-2, SC-3) are provided in Appendix A to assist you.

Each day can take on a different schedule, or you may have two or three days with the same schedule. Remember, as the week progresses, you will spend more time in mass rehearsals and less time in classes. At the beginning of camp, start with five tentative schedules, one for each day. The Monday schedule should be solid, but all other days are subject to change, depending on need. Answering the following questions can help you begin to make some important decisions about the camp agenda.

Questions and Considerations

- Will there be Early Bird activities before camp begins?
- Will there be an Opening Assembly with games, skits, and activities for the first 20 minutes of camp?
- Will you purchase recordings of the musical and mail them to the campers to review before camp starts?
- If campers are familiar with the musical, class time can be approximately 20 minutes. If, however, the music is totally unfamiliar, class time will need to be at least 30-45 minutes.

Let me reiterate: ordering the practice recordings takes tremendous pressure off the week and frees the schedule to include more activities. Singing is great fun, but it makes for a laborious schedule when children spend several full days just learning new music. The practice recordings are definitely worth the extra expense!

- Will the camp be divided into teams? If so, how many? For instance, if there are four teams, at least four or more classes must be planned.
- How will classes be structured? What types of classes will be offered? Examples: crafts, Bible study, activity class, recorders or Orff instruments, recreation, music theory, team quizzes.

SURVIVAL TiP

Remember, as the week progresses, you will spend more time in mass rehearsals and less time in classes.

- If camp runs all day, will there be a morning and an afternoon snack time? Will there be one lunch period or two; and, how much time will be allotted for lunch? (I suggest 20-30 minutes for lunch with a bathroom break.) Will you provide lunch or will the children bring their own?
- Will the children sit with their teams at lunch, or will there be open seating? We have fewer problems when children continue to sit with their group leaders and teams.
- It is always wise to schedule bathroom breaks before a mass rehearsal to reduce the number of children asking to leave. Assigning the teams to individual bathrooms throughout the church will expedite these breaks.
- Will you schedule a costume class? During this class, individual children can be measured for costumes. This could possibly be combined with a refreshment class. Some camps allow the children to help make their own costumes as part of an activity class. Different teams can do different costume projects that can be fun and helpful to the production. If camp T-shirts and pants are used as stage dress, a costume class may not be necessary.
- Will you want to schedule a time to work with your lead characters and soloists? This would work well when the majority of campers are in a recreation class. In my own camps, I try not to teach a class on Tuesday morning. This allows freedom to call children out of class and work with them individually if they have solos or speaking parts.
- How much time will be needed to close out the day? Will there be an afternoon feature or closing assembly? Will daily awards be given or a special treat be served? Above all, this should be an organized time because it is very visible to the parents. There is so much potential for chaos. Have some quiet group games ready. Have a special room where staff children can go during dismissal. This is very helpful in determining when all regular campers have been picked up. Camp staff can then go get their own children.
- Will you need to schedule a time for pictures during the week? Make these plans early and work out all logistics of placement for the actual photo shoot.
- Will you be planning a carnival? What day and time? Who will coordinate this event?
- Will you have a refreshment class built into your daily schedule or will you serve everyone at the same time? In addition to a regular lunch time, we have cookies and drink in the morning and snow cones in the afternoon.

Sample Camp Schedules

Hopefully, after answering these questions, you will have a better idea of how to structure your camp. The following samples can help you work through several different schedules. These schedules are simply suggestions to give guidance and help you make

---

Design the schedule to fit your specific needs and desires as well as fulfill your ministry goals.

---

some choices. Be aware that these are only one-day examples. As the week progresses, you will need fewer classes and more mass rehearsals to pull the musical together. The following schedules have no real travel time built in between classes. Keep this in mind as you plan.

Several blank scheduling forms are provided in Appendix A to assist you in this process, or you may want to create one of your own.

Example A is for a 9 a.m.–3 p.m. camp. This camp is divided into six teams. There are 7 classes in the morning schedule/track. You will need 7 teachers to lead the classes. Each class is 20 minutes. If campers are familiar with the music, a 20-minute music class should be adequate. During the first mass rehearsal, practice only the songs that the children learned in the morning classes.

In the afternoon, there are three classes with three teachers in which two teams are now combined in one class at a time.

Suggestions for this time:
- Teach the slower, less active songs.
- Teach 2 simpler, shorter songs.
- Bible quizzing works well with 2 teams because they can compete with each other.
- This is also a great time for recreation if you have somewhere that is cool and out of the hot sun.

This type of schedule allows for teachers that can only come in the morning to help. After 12:00, they are free to go home when only three teachers are needed in the afternoon.

8:00 a.m...............Staff Meeting/ Coffee and doughnuts; Child care open
8:40-9:00...................Early Bird Activities
9:00-9:10.....................Opening Assembly (introductions, character lesson, theme song or Scripture verse)
9:10-9:30.............Music Class 1
9:30-9:50.............Music Class 2
9:50-10:10...........Music Class 3
10:10-10:30.........Music Class 4
10:30-10:50......Bible study or Quiz; Activity or Craft class (Class 5)
10:50-11:10...Snack/Recreation
11:10 -11:40.......Stage Class— placing children on stage (Class 6)
11:40 a.m -12:15 p.m........Mass Rehearsal
12:15-12:45...Lunch/Bathroom
12:45-1:05..........Music Class A
1:05-1:25.............Music Class B
1:25-1:45.............Bible study or Quiz; Activity or Craft Class; Recreation (Class C)
1:45-1:55.......Bathroom Break
1:55-2:30..........Mass Rehearsal
2:30-2:50...................Afternoon Feature (snow cones and awards, closing assembly, and so forth.)
2:50-3:05..........Parents pick up campers
3:30.................Staff children's room and child care closed

Example B is for a 9 a.m.–3 p.m. camp. This camp is divided into six teams. There are six classes in the morning schedule/track; therefore, six teachers are needed to lead 30-minute classes. In this schedule, there is not time for a mass rehearsal before lunch. For travel time, make each class 25 minutes with five minutes in between.

8:00 a m..............Staff Meeting/ Coffee and doughnuts; Child care open
8:30-8:45...................Early Bird Activities
8:45-9:00.....................Opening Assembly (introductions, character lesson, theme song or Scripture verse)
9:00-9:30.............Music Class 1
9:30-10:00...........Music Class 2
10:00-10:30.........Music Class 3
10:30-11:00.........Music Class 4
11:00-11:30.......Bible study or Quiz; Activity or Craft Class; recreation (Class 5)
11:30-a.m.-12:00 p.m......Stage Class—placing children on stage (Class 6)
12:00-12:30...Lunch/Bathroom
12:30-1:00..........Music Class A
1:00-1:30.............Music Class B
1:30-2:00.............Bible study or Quiz; Activity or Craft Class; Recreation (Class C)
2:00-2:30..........Mass Rehearsal
2:30-3:00...................Afternoon Feature (snow cones and awards, closing assembly, and so forth.)
3:00.....Parents pick up campers
3:30.......Staff children's room and child care closed

Example C is for a 9 a.m.–3 p.m. camp. This camp is divided into six teams. Instead of having a morning schedule and a different afternoon schedule as in Examples A and B, this one has an all-day track. There are 8 classes that run all day; therefore, you will need 8 teachers to lead the 30-minute classes. This schedule requires all teachers to work all day. Also, there is not a mass rehearsal before lunch because the children will not have attended every class time until after the 1:00 p.m. class.

8:00 a.m..............Staff Meeting/ Coffee and doughnuts; Child care open
8:30-8:45...................Early Bird Activities
8:45-9:00......................Opening Assembly (introductions, character lesson, theme song or Scripture verse)
9:00-9:30.............Class 1-Music
9:30-10:00...........Class 2-Music
10:00-10:30........Class 3-Music
10:30-11:00........Class 4-Music
11:00-11:30..........Class 5-Bible study or Quiz, Activity or Craft Class, Recreation
11:30 a.m.-12:00 p.m.....Class 6 Stage Class (placing children on stage)
12:00-12:30...Lunch/Bathroom
12:30-1:00..........Class 7-Music
1:00-1:30........... Class 8-Music
1:30-2:30.........Mass Rehearsal
2:30-3:00...................Afternoon Feature (snow cones and awards; closing assembly)
3:00.....Parents pick up campers
3:30........Staff children's room and child care closed

Example D is for a 3-hour camp whether it is in the morning or evening. You will need to have at least the same number of classes as you do teams. If you have six or fewer teams in your camp, the schedule could look like this.

8:00 a.m..............Staff Meeting/ Coffee and doughnuts; Child care open
8:30-8:45....................Early Bird Activities
8:45-9:00......................Opening Assembly (introductions, character lesson, theme song or Scripture verse)
9:00-9:20.............Music Class 1
9:20-9:40.............Music Class 2
9:40-10:00..........Music Class 3
10:00-10:20........Music Class 4
10:20-10:40....Snack/Bathroom
10:40-11:00.......Bible study or Quiz; Activity or Craft Class; recreation (Class 5)
11:00-11:20.............Stage Class (Class 6)
11:20-11:50.......Mass rehearsal
11:50 a.m.-12:00 p.m. Closing activity
12:00..........................Dismissal
12:30...............Staff children's room and child care closed

Example E is an evening schedule option with 20 minute classes.

5:30 p.m.-6:00 p.m...........Light supper for campers, Early Bird activities as needed.
6:00-6:20.............Music Class 1
6:20-6:40.............Music Class 2
6:40-7:00.............Music Class 3
7:00-7:20.............Music Class 4
7:20-7:40.............Class 5: Bible study or Quiz; Activity or Craft Class; Recreation
7:40-8:00.............Class 6: Stage Class and bathroom break
8:00 -8:25..........Mass rehearsal
8:25-8:30.........Closing, awards, and dismissal

Example F is an evening, 2.5-hour camp that is feasible but more difficult. If you have six teams, then six, 20-minute classes will completely fill your schedule. If you extend to 8:30, you can have a mass rehearsal.

5:30 p.m.-6:00 p.m...........Early Bird activities, sport type activities, and snack followed by an opening assembly
6:00-6:20.............Music Class 1
6:20-6:40.............Music Class 2
6:40-7:00.............Music Class 3
7:00-7:20.............Music Class 4
7:20-7:40.............Class 5: Bible study or Quiz; Activity or Craft Class; Recreation
7:40-8:00.............Class 6: Stage Class and bathroom break
8:00........................*Dismissal

*optional 8:00-8:30...Mass Rehearsal followed by dismissal.

SAMPLE INDIVIDUAL TEAM SCHEDULES

Monday's Schedule would begin as follows:

8:30-9:00 a.m. Early Bird Activities

		Class 1	Class 2	Class 3	Class 4	Class 5	Class 6
9:00-9:30	Blue Bears (BB)	(YY)	(RR)	(PP)	(OO)	(GG)
9:30-10:00	Green Giraffes (GG)	(BB)	(YY)	(RR)	(PP)	(OO)
10:00-10:30	Orange Orangutans (OO)	(GG)	(BB)	(YY)	(RR)	(PP)
10:30-11:00	Purple Pandas (PP)	(OO)	(GG)	(BB)	(YY)	(RR)
11:00-11:30	Red (RR)	(PP)	(OO)	(GG)	(BB)	(YY)
11:30-12:00	Yellow Yaks (YY)	(RR)	(PP)	(OO)	(GG)	(BB)

12:00-12:30 p.m. Lunch and Bathroom Break

     All group leaders will take the children's lunches to the Fellowship Hall and help set up.

     Adult group leaders eat with children. Youth group leaders' get lunch break.

	Class A	Class B	Class C
12:30-1:00	Teams BB and GG	Teams RR and YY	Teams OO and PP
1:00-1:30	Teams OO and PP	Teams BB and GG	Teams RR and YY
1:30-2:00	Teams RR and YY	Teams OO and PP	Teams BB and GG

2:00-2:10	Bathroom Break
2:10-2:40	Mass Rehearsal – Auditorium
2:40-3:00	Snow Cones & Awards
3:00	Parents pick up campers
3:30	Staff children picked up

Example G is the same 2.5-hour schedule but divides the camp into 4 teams.

5:30 p.m.-6:00 p.m...........Early Bird activities, sport type activities, and snack followed by an opening assembly

6:00-6:20.............Music Class 1

6:20-6:40.............Music Class 2

6:40-7:00......Music Class 3 and place the children on stage

7:00-7:20.............Class 4: Bible study or Quiz; Activity or Craft Class; Recreation

7:20-7:55...........Mass rehearsal

7:55-8:00................Awards and dismissal

Class Decisions

More Questions

•Will your afternoon classes be a continuation of the morning? For example, will you have Classes 1, 2, 3, 4 in the morning and after lunch, Classes 6,7, and 8? If you choose to have one track for all day, a morning mass rehearsal will not be possible because not every group will have learned the same songs until the end of the day. To avoid this complication, choose to have a morning schedule where all the children complete the cycle of classes before lunch. Then, have a different afternoon schedule. For example, Classes 1, 2, 3, 4, 5, and 6 are in the morning. After lunch, start a new track of classes A, B, C.

•Will there be a music class for every song in the musical? Sometimes two easier songs can be combined in one class. We suggest learning the hardest songs with choreography in the morning. Afternoon is a good time to learn the easier songs with less choreography. We sometimes combine two teams together and have fewer classes in the afternoon.

•Will you want to schedule an individual class (Stage Class) for the Musical Director to place the children on stage while in smaller groups?
This would only be necessary on the first day of camp. It is far less confusing this way than trying to place the entire camp on stage at a mass rehearsal.

•How many Music Teachers will be needed to teach the songs?
Remember, a camp Music Teacher doesn't have to have a degree to teach a song. Youth do well at teaching. If a person can sing well with a recording and has energy, he or she can teach a song. Pianos are not always necessary; CD/tape players are sufficient. If you are wanting to teach music education with every song, that would demand a different kind of teacher. Divide the songs among the Music Teachers rather than having a separate teacher for each song. A word of advice, do not overload volunteer teachers with more than one or two songs.

•If you have an all-day camp, will you plan a mass rehearsal on the first day?
Some camps have only classes the first and second day. I strongly advise getting the children on stage for a mass rehearsal that first day, twice if possible. Mass rehearsals will vary every day. They should last 45 minutes to an hour.

•Will you have a craft class? Do you have a creative staff person to take this area?
Make sure the crafts enhance the message of the musical.

•Will you have an activity class or a Bible study class?
Use the musical Scripture references for Bible study. The director's guide might provide suggestions for activities.

•Will you have a recreation class?
Mass recreation classes are more difficult to control, but to play some group games, you may need a large size group. A team recreation class is another option. Place two teams in a class, and this creates a nice size group that works well for relays and other competitive games.

•Is there a good area for recreation at the church? Is there a person that is gifted in this area to be on the camp staff?
Think about an alternate plan in case of bad weather. Will there be recreation every day or only on certain days? Recreation is a nice

class to have in the afternoon if you have a gymnasium. Whether you choose recreation or not, it is always a good idea to have at least one great game in your pocket for emergencies.

Some camps allow campers to choose between a craft class, recreation class, or activity class. Extra camp staff might be necessary to accommodate this option.

•Will you have a Bible quizzing class?
Because of the practice involved in Bible quizzing, this class needs to be scheduled in the morning and in the afternoon (i.e. twice a day). In the morning class, children learn the Scriptures. In the afternoon, they practice with a quiz machine and another team. (This class option is discussed in more detail later in this chapter.)

•Do you want to have a music theory class or will you incorporate this into your regular music classes?
Theory material is sometimes available through the teacher's guide. See Appendix E for additional resources.

Class Content Ideas
Music Class
These classes should be designed to teach the songs in the musical as well as the choreography. Each teacher should teach approximately two songs, depending on difficulty.

Character Corner

We have chosen four character qualities to emphasize during our camp. You may use these or choose others that will encourage the campers to display their best behavior during the music camp week.

Attentiveness

This means to listen to others and pay strict attention, especially to camp leaders and teachers. It also means to be aware of others and have a desire to listen to them. Be alert!
Use Mark 4:23-24 as a Scripture reference.

We begin with attentiveness Monday morning at 9:00 a.m. When a teacher holds her hands up with her pointer fingers pointed up, this is our attention sign. It means get quiet and listen with immediate silence! Campers should give their undivided attention, and show it in their expression, eyes, and body language.
Signs of attentiveness are:
• heads up
• eyes open wide
• Campers can nod their heads to agree with what is being said.
• good posture
• mouths closed
• hands and feet still
I play a game with the campers to see how quickly they can get quiet and attentive. I look for children who are good examples of this character quality and ask them to show their attentive-

ness in front of others. You may also have contests between the groups to see who can show attentiveness the best.

Obedience

This means immediately doing what you are told to do with a great attitude and being happy to do what is right. Use Exodus 24:7; Acts 5:29; Ephesians 6:1; Colossians 3:20; and Jonah 1:1-5; 3:1-3,10 as possible Scripture references.

Campers should
• support the team, and be a good team member
• have the right attitude
• learn the songs and choreography
• play hard and have a great time
• act correctly on stage without bothering others
• stay in class during class time
• pick up their trash and clean up after themselve.
• keep up with belongings
• be at presentations on time, in costume
• wear name tags correctly

Responsibility

This means to know and do what God, leaders, and fellow campers expect.
It is important for children to understand that God, their parents, and the music camp staff are expecting and trusting them to personally be responsible for doing what is right. Some of the Scriptures for obedience, addressed pre-

viously, or trust, mentioned later, may be useful for this character trait as well.

Enthusiasm

This means giving 100 percent all the time, and then some. What a concept! Help children learn to give all they can and then give some more. What are some characteristics of an enthusiastic person?

Children should demonstrate
• whole-hearted singing
• energy when doing motions
• being quiet yet enthusiastic on stage while a scene is taking place
• picking up the trash or obeying any simple task with a willing spirit
I have seen children respond with and without enthusiasm. I would never embarrass a child by pointing out his lack of enthusiasm, but I might bring a similar situation back for discussion at a later time, not pointing out the individual, but asking the campers to help evaluate or correct it. Use Romans 12:11 as a Scripture reference.

We often find individual stories to use with each character quality. Some involve animals, others examine an athlete or Bible character. For example, name a person in the Bible who showed responsibility and obedience *(Noah)*. Even though everyone was laughing at him, he kept right on building the ark and doing what God told him to do. He had character qualities of responsibility and obedience. It is always good to relate any character story to the musical being studied. There are many other wonderful character qualities that are available to use, but we have chosen these four because they help specifically focus on camp behavior.

Other characteristics worthy of presenting are love, patience, and trust. The following Scripture references relate to these traits:

- *Love:*
  Leviticus 19:18
  Matthew 5:43-44
  John 13:34
  1 John 4:7
- *Patience:*
  Psalm 40:1
  Ecclesiastes 7:8
  Matthew 18:26
- *Trust:*
  Psalm 37:3
  Psalm 56:3
  Proverbs 3:5
  Daniel, chapters 1, 2, 3, 6

You can schedule a Character Corner class, but we present "Character Moments" all week. These are short breaks when a character story is appropriate, such as during Opening or Closing Assembly.

Here are some suggestions for Character Corner resources:
- Ask your pastor or youth and children's ministers.
- Use examples from character related curriculum or books.
- Home schooling families are a good source for character books.

- Christian schools in the area may have material to lend.
- Stories of great Christians or missionaries may be in your church library.
- The best source is your Bible.

Remind the camp staff that in order to build these attributes in the camper's lives, the children must see it in their authority figures first.

Activity Class
This class can be theme-related to the musical, music theory oriented, a composer study, or extra work on choreography. If you have access to copies of *Made for Praise®*, or *Children's Music Series™ Quarterly Curriculum* products from LifeWay Church Resources, they are always full of games and activities. Be creative, there are so many possibilities!

Craft Class
This could involve costume design, work on scenery, theme-related banners, or just a fun time of various crafts.

Recreation/Sports
This can be structured or non-structured free play, organized games, team building exercises, and so forth.

Bible Study
Director's Guides often provide activities for this class. Enlist a pastor or children's minister to lead studies of the Scriptures related to the musical.

Bible Quizzing
One of the very best parts of our camps has been quizzing on Scripture passages. There are Bible quizzing manuals and videos on the market. We encourage you to get a manual and video to discover the fun and the different ways this game can be used in your church.

Most musicals emphasize a passage of Scripture or several individual Scriptures that support the story line. For example, *Nic at Night* focused on John 3:1-18. It was our desire to emphasize Scripture as much as the music, but how can that be done in one short week with so many other activities? When we found a Bible quizzing game, we had our answer!

Bible Quizzing Details

Method and Equipment
This should be a game that is similar to the TV game show, *Jeopardy*. Instead of a buzzer that you hit with your hand, we have the children sit on seat pads. When a question is asked, the object is to be the first person to come off of the seat pad. Each pad is connected to a master panel that sits on a table and is battery powered. The numbers 1-20 on the panel have a corresponding light and switch. If a child is the first to come off of the seat pad, his corresponding light will go off. If he answers the question correctly, his team gets a point. If he cannot answer the question correctly, the teacher switches

off his light on the panel, then the light of the child who was second to come off the set pad will light up. The teacher will then repeat the question and ask that child to answer.

This should be a game designed to take a passage of Scripture and ask very detailed questions about the passage. Choose someone on your camp staff who is a gifted teacher for the responsibility of writing the questions. Divide the questions into three groups. Monday, Tuesday, and Wednesday, the children learn a new group of questions each day. These questions can be in the newsletter for that day so the children can practice at home. The quizzing machine should be set up in a classroom where campers can practice with it, usually twice a day.

Please understand, this particular activity is primarily dependent upon the equipment used to run the game. However, I am aware of a music camp in another state that could not afford the equipment their first year. They loved the concept, though, and decided to make it work for their camp without the equipment. Although the purchase will be a major expense, the quiz machine can be used with so many other groups. It might be possible that your church would divide the cost between several other ministries.

The following web sites will help you gain access to equipment for Bible quizzing games:
- quiztime.com
- quizsystems.com
- biblequiz.com
- quizbot.com
- zeecraft.com

Use these for equipment, but develop questions for the game from the musical you are teaching.

Rules
A team gets one point for each correct answer. If a child answers three correct questions during a round, he "quizzes out" and everyone cheers as he sits down and is replaced with another team member. It is the goal of every team member to quiz out. A player is given an error if called on and unable to give the correct answer. If a player receives three errors, she is quietly asked to take a seat. At our camp, we compete by ages to try to make the games more even. For example, one round would involve all the six-year-olds from each team. The next round would be all the seven and eight-year-olds from each team.

With six camp groups, (Blue Bears, Orange Orangutans, etc.) each group sends three children of the same age. There is an eight-minute round with each age group.

Competition
We make a big deal of the "Big Bible Quiz Off" on Thursday. We invite the parents to come, and the auditorium is always full. Make sure to explain the procedure for the parents so that they understand the game. Have the equipment and chairs set on stage so everyone can see. Provide a microphone for the teacher who will ask the questions. A table should be set up off stage (down in front of the children's chairs) where the quizzing teacher and assistant will sit, and the panel box is set up. Each team can cheer for their players when they make a point. However, it is very important that things are quiet during the questions.

The winner of the Quiz Off is not announced that day. After the Friday night presentation of the musical, medals are awarded to each member of the winning team. The second place team is also recognized and asked to stand. The medals are placed around the winning team members' necks in an Olympic style ceremony. It's so much fun! We order the medals from a trophy shop, but do not put individual names on the medals. We use the following engraving:
Summer Music Camp
Bible Quiz Champs 2002
We truly believe this quizzing game is a tool to help the children hide God's Word in their hearts.

Purpose
The primary purpose for this game has just been stated in the previous sentence. However, I've asked myself the

question, "Why does the Bible quizzing work so well for our camp?" I think there are several reasons. First, I believe God has blessed this activity. Psalm 1:1-3 states, "How happy is the man who does not follow the advice of the wicked, or take the path of sinners...Instead, his delight is in the Lord's instruction, and he meditates on it day and night. He is like a tree planted beside streams of water that bears its fruit in season and whose leaf does not wither."

Secondly, it is a fun, high intensity game where children can play against their own team members or the entire camp. This helps build real team spirit among children regardless of their ages. Outside of the preparation of the quiz teacher, the setting up of equipment, and the preparing of the questions, this is a major thrust of our camp that demands very little preparation from other staff, and yet everyone is highly involved. When you choose to have several other major classes, it is just that much more preparation on that many more teachers. The quizzing game is our major Bible emphasis, and that emphasis has taken away part of the pressure and stress of trying to plan other major classes.

A sister church borrowed our quizzing machine one summer for their music camp. After seeing the fun, they ordered one immediately for their next camp. Check with some larger churches in your area to see if they have a quiz machine before ordering.

Other Activities

Spirit Stick
The Spirit Stick is a way of rewarding the team that has the best attitude and exhibits the character qualities of attentiveness, obedience, responsibility, and enthusiasm. (Love, patience, and trust could also be added to this list depending on the characteristics being emphasized.)
The stick itself can be made from a broom handle. Paint it red, white, and blue for patriotism, or use solid purple to symbolize royalty. A psychedelic yellow would also be bold and quite visible. Keep it the same every year, or change it to fit your musical. Decorate one end with something ornate or add ribbon streamers. Use your imagination!

We display the Spirit Stick on Monday morning right after the first character lesson. Share with the campers what is required to win the Spirit Stick. All staff members (except Group Leaders) will look for the team that does the best job during the day's activities, considering these elements, for example: attitude, listening instead of talking, showing enthusiasm and participation,

behavior at lunch time and other special activities, cleaning up lunch table, and so on.

At the close of the day, each staff member gives their vote to an assigned teacher. Whichever group has the most votes wins the Spirit Stick. Make a big deal of it. At the Closing Assembly, do a drum roll with great anticipation. Appoint a staff person who can "ham it up" to award the Spirit Stick. The winning group will carry the Spirit Stick around with them the next day.

The process starts again on Tuesday morning, and on Tuesday afternoon, the Spirit Stick is awarded again. It can be awarded to the same group or a new group. We award the Spirit Stick Monday through Thursday afternoons.

A Carnival
Our church had done several carnival-type activities in our community. Because the games were already made, we decided it was a perfect addition to our camp. The games are simple to make, and the children just love a carnival. We usually have our carnival outside and start early in the day because of the heat. We begin around 10:00 a.m. on Wednesday and end about noon. If you have good shade, you should be fine. We have also had the carnival inside our gym on Wednesday afternoon. Outside, you deal with the heat. Inside, you deal with

the noise level.

Teachers and Group Leaders help organize the games while the Director is in a mass rehearsal from 9:00–10:00 a.m. Each Group Leader gives each child in her group a small paper sack with the child's name and a color-coded dot. These sacks sometimes get lost and the color-coded dot will indicate the group to which it belongs. On each paper sack, we staple two tickets. The tickets are for the Bounce-a-Round game. Any other game can be played as much as possible.

Carnival Considerations

If you choose to have a carnival during your week, order prizes early. Companies such as U. S. Toys®, Oriental Trading®, or Abbey Press® usually sell in bulk. Big packages of small individual candy from a food warehouse can also be used as prizes. If games need to be built, this should be started early as well. We have a party store in our area that has some carnival-type games that rent for a few dollars each. These are great additions to a carnival and very reasonable. We also rented a cotton candy machine and a dunking machine from a large rental store. All of these items required a small deposit to hold them for our carnival date.

There are companies that will come and set up a complete carnival. We know a company that will provide inflatable

slides and moonwalks, kiddie rides, booths, concessions, and prizes. This is much more expensive, but this type of service is available. You can also rent individual rides and games. Check the local yellow pages for this type of service, and remember that dates must be secured early.

Bounce-a-Round

This inflatable jumping room has been a real addition to our carnival. Children can jump as many times as they wish, but children with tickets get to go in first. By the end of the carnival, most kids are jumping without a ticket, but the tickets ensure each child of getting to jump at least twice. The owner allows only a certain number of children in the structure at a time, for safety reasons. The children will jump for a while, and then a new group will jump. The children keep lining up and jumping until the carnival is over.

The owner of the equipment stays a bit longer and allows our youth to have a turn. They give so much during the week. It is nice to do something special for them.

SURVIVAL TIP

There are companies that will come and set up a complete carnival. Check the local yellow pages for this type of service, and remember that dates must be secured early.

It is important that the camp staff take part in the fun activities of the week. It is good for children to see the adults laugh, act silly, enjoy being with the children, and playing the games.

Games

Here are some carnival game suggestions. Be creative and adjust this list to meet your needs.

Cake (Candy) Walk

You need carpet squares, a tape player, music, candy, and small, individual, pre-packaged cakes. Children must walk in a circle on the carpet squares. When the music is stopped, a number is drawn from a hat; that number wins the cake. Everyone else gets a piece of candy.

Basketball Game

Throw a ball into a trash can or a hoop. This can easily be a child's basketball goal brought from home.

Ducks in Water

A child's small pool filled with water, plastic ducks with one that says prize. Each child gets a small prize; a slightly larger prize goes to the winner.

Ping Pong Balls in a Bucket

You need five plastic buckets of the same size. They can be painted or covered in a colored foil or wrapping paper. Buckets are lined up vertically in front of the child. The child is given five ping pong balls and is to get one ball in each bucket to win.

Paint Sticks

The game is played like *Horseshoes*. Purchase paint sticks, which may cost ten cents each, from any paint store. Spray the paint sticks a bright color. Stick them in the ground vertically. Use vacuum cleaner rings and throw a ring around each stick.

Go Fishing Game

Use a fishing pole or a bamboo pole with a long string and a basket on the end of the string. A staff person will stand behind a divider or backboard and put a prize in the basket for each child as he/she lowers it over the dividend. This backboard can be decorated with fish net.

Hand or Face Painting

We paint on hands instead of faces because Wednesday is also picture day. Either way, this can easily be washed off. You can purchase face paint and extra brushes at most discount stores. Youth staffers love to take this post at the carnival.

One year, I called a local party shop and asked if they had any carnival games we could rent. They had six different games, which added to our carnival fun. They were very inexpensive to rent for the day. We've even considered adding pony rides. Use your creativity! Carnival games do not have to be complex to be fun.

Food

Hot dogs, mustard, ketchup, relish, popcorn, cookies, and Kool-Aid® are on the menu. (See the Carnival Coordinator job description section in Chapter 4 for food specifics.)

Children can come and get food starting at 11:00 a.m. If the weather is hot, be sure to have a big container of water and plenty of cups. Provide several large trash cans as well.

Set up the food under a big

tent to give some shade. Teachers, group leaders, and other staff take turns doing the games and refreshments. When it is time to go in, the campers pick up trash and put their prize sacks in color-coded buckets.

It is important that your leadership and staff take part in the fun activities of the week. It is good for children to see the adults laugh, act silly, enjoy being with the children, and playing the games. There is a special bond when you are making wonderful memories. Moreover, the church will represent a place where people truly love and care for others. When these children are grown, they may need some type of special help. It is our prayer that they will remember these special times and have the freedom to come back to the church for godly answers.

Final Preparations

Sunday Before Camp
The teachers set up their rooms; have a CD player available to them. Clear the stage and set up for the week. Arrange the orange traffic cones with the team posters down the aisles. Set up the registration tables with the needed supplies. Someone should get the coffee ready to plug in early!

One of the most special things we do to prepare for music camp is to have the camp staff come to the altar at the close of the service the Sunday night before camp starts on Monday. The deacons and the whole church body go to the altar to pray for us. It is a very humbling and empowering time. It is a reminder to the entire church to keep the staff and children in their prayers.

After the service, there is a brief staff meeting just to touch base and finalize any loose ends. Remind everyone of the camp mission statement and that flexibility should be the theme song for the week. Sometimes there are staff members who could not make it for the first meeting and they may have some questions at this time. Keep this meeting short and pray again before dismissal.

Monday Morning
The Camp Director(s) should be at the church early. The auditorium and classrooms need to be checked to see that

SURVIVAL TiP

Prepare for music camp by having a camp staff dedication at the close of a Sunday night service before camp begins.

Church leadership joins the staff and leads the congregation in prayer. This will remind the entire church to keep the camp in their prayers.

the air conditioner has been turned on. The Kitchen Coordinator needs to have coffee, milk, and doughnuts ready for the staff and staff children by 7:50 a.m. The staff children's room needs to be staffed and ready by 7:50 a.m., perhaps with a TV and VCR, board games, simple activities, and coloring sheets. Child care workers need to be ready by 7:50 a.m. to receive any babies and toddlers. The sound system in the auditorium should be turned on and a microphone ready for the Early Bird activities. At 7:50 a.m., the staff children need to go to the child care room or the staff children's room.

At 8:00 a.m., the daily staff meeting should begin. Answer any last-minute questions; briefly go over the policies one more time; pray as a group; and then get ready to welcome the campers! See the staff section of this manual in Chapter 4 for further details of this meeting.

One Group Leader from each team should stay in the auditorium with the registered campers when they arrive. The other Group Leaders need to greet the new campers as they leave the registration table to join the Early Bird activities. At 8:40 a.m., the Early Bird Activities begin. The Group Leaders and extra teachers should participate to encourage the fun atmosphere. At 9:00 a.m., the Camp/Musical Director, the

pastor, or a church staff member gives an official welcome. Teach a quick Character Lesson on attentiveness. Show off the Spirit Stick and explain that at the end of the day, the teachers will be voting on which group has the best attitude and is the most attentive. The Camp Director introduces each group and the Group Leaders. Then, one group at a time, campers quietly follow their leaders out of the auditorium to their assigned classrooms. It is important to stay on schedule!

SURVIVAL TIP

It is important to stay on schedule! This will eliminate many nitpicky problems.

chapter 4
THE STAFF

help lead an activity class; and, you can ask for volunteers from parents to help during lunch.

Another option is to plan a camp that doesn't include lunch, and eliminate the need for those extra workers. If uncertain about enough help, start with a three-hour camp that primarily involves music and staging. If you feel more confident the next year, expand to a six-hour camp and add more of the day-camp type activities. As parents and others see the value of what you are doing, more volunteers will appear.

A "Bare-Boned" Staff

When planning your camp, have an idea who will be working with you during the week. The unique gifts of each will help determine what classes and activities to plan for the campers. Most of our staff are at camp eight to nine hours a day. Some workers come to help only during lunch or with registration. We have others that help during the Early Bird activities and with child care before 9:00 a.m.; then, they leave and go to their regular jobs. What a blessing to have such committed staff.

There have been times; however, as our next camp approached, workers would begin to say they would not be able to help. For whatever rea-

sons they had and regardless of how understanding I felt, there's a tendency to panic at the thought of not having enough staff. However, these basic questions summarize the proverbial bottom line. If the frills are cut, can all bases be covered? What is the "bare-boned" staff that must be in place for the week to succeed?

This section is written to encourage you. Even though you may not have anywhere near the number of staff listed here, you can still have an outstanding camp with only a small number of workers. Plan your days to fit your workers. Don't worry about all the extras, just cover the basics! The Camp Director can teach the songs and the choreography; one or two teachers can

In addition, it is important to protect the spirit of the camp. Discuss all camp staff responsibilities with your pastor or music minister before camp begins. Work out details ahead of time to avoid any problems or frustrations during the week.

Potential Staff List
(A forward slash / indicates positions that can be combinations or separate staff positions.)

- Camp Director
- Musical Director
- Registration Director/ Camp Secretary
- Finance Director
- Group Leaders (Adults and Youth)
- Music Teachers
- Drama/ Choreography Coordinator
- Accompanist

Plan your camp days to fit your workers. If you have a bare-bones staff you can still have an outstanding camp. Don't worry about all the extras— just cover the basics!

- Early Bird Activity/ Opening Assembly Coordinator
- Recreation Coordinator and Leaders
- Bible Quiz Leader
- Activity/Craft Leaders
- Prop and Staging Manager
- Kitchen Coordinator and Aides
- Reception Coordinator
- Carnival Coordinator
- Child Care Coordinator and Workers
- Camp Nurse
- Advertising and Publicity/ Newsletter Editor
- Camp Videographer/ Photographer
- Janitor

Staff Responsibilities

(Permission is granted to duplicate these job descriptions for staff members.)

Camp Director

My husband and I are co-directors at our camp. This makes for a great arrangement because we share all responsibilities. We work well as a team and have a lot of fun leading together.

Another idea is to have a Camp Director and a Musical Director. There are so many details involved in the camp planning. A non-musical person could take those responsibilities which would involve registration, mailings, special activities, schedules, staff, etc. The Musical Director would deal with special parts, rehearsals, costumes, staging, music, choreography, etc. It is still a good idea to have a church staff person (e.g. minister of music) oversee these two positions just to give leadership, and help in the direction of the week.

In every team, whether it's two people or five people, there has to be a leader. If a group of churches is working together to produce a music camp, make sure it is understood who, ultimately, has the final word on all decisions. If leadership is undefined, the creativity and organization of your camp will suffer.

Whether you share the responsibilities of the directorship or work in this position alone, the Camp Director is in charge of, and responsible for, the following:
- securing the major dates
- choosing the classes and creating the camp agenda
- making decisions concerning registration, fees, and finances

It is the Camp Director's job to constantly focus the camp, make every activity more organized, change what does not work, and enhance what should be emphasized.

- advertising and publicity
- mailing list and mailings
- ordering books, tapes/CDs, and T-shirts

- recruiting staff
- building and/or ordering new equipment
- checking to see that the church building is prepared for camp (classrooms, stage, lawn, etc.)
- public relations with the staff, campers, and parents
- carnival games and prizes
- T-shirt and video sales
- distributing videos
- writing thank-you notes
- follow-up
- bringing the camp to a close, including finances
- whatever else needs to be done
- The responsibilities of the Musical Director, if there isn't one, will fall to the Camp Director as well.

To keep from being over-whelmed, remember that *any of these areas can, and should, be delegated to other responsible people.* Some, though, are so important that they may need the Director's individual attention.
This manual is designed to make the director's job much easier. Every item above is addressed in this manual. It will serve as the guide through the planning stages as well as the actual camp.

One of the most important responsibilities of the Camp Director is recruiting the staff. This chapter has a section for staff workers to read, describing their positions and responsibilities. If there is a need to combine responsibilities for the week, a worker is given all of the written sections that are

SAFETY RULES AND PROCEDURES

- Children must be six years old by September 1 (entering first grade) to be a part of music camp.

- All purchased camp items must be prepaid. If items are not prepaid, you may be looking months later at boxes of unclaimed videos, T-shirts, and pictures, not to mention the bill!

- Children are not to wear hats to music camp. If head lice have not been a problem in your community, you are blessed. If a child does wear a hat to camp, take it and place in a plastic bag, tie a knot in the bag, and place the bag in the child's color-coded basket or tub. The child can take the hat home at the end of the day.

- Bathing suits should not be worn to camp. Shorts and T-shirts are fine for any water activities that are planned.

- We ask that parents not send sack lunches that must be refrigerated. There are cold packs that can be purchased inexpensively to keep items cool. Each camper should bring individual sacks or lunch boxes, rather than one per family.

- Parents should check with the Camp Director or office if they need to take a child out of camp before the end of the day. This is to reduce confusion and, more importantly, ensure the safety of the child.

- In case of an emergency, be sure the staff is informed. Discuss with the staff what to do in case of a fire, tornado warning, or any other emergency. Group Leaders should have an exact count of the children in their group. Have a first aid kit with plastic gloves, clean towels, and someone to be a nurse that has the understanding of how to handle emergency situations. Be sure that you have phone numbers (home and work) where a parent or guardian can be reached during the day. Also, know where to take a child in case of a medical emergency. Check the church's insurance policy before an emergency happens.

appropriate to his or her position(s). If a camp schedule is chosen that does not use one of these positions, disregard it.

As you begin to plan your camp, use the staff responsibility pages as a guide. In the

early stages of planning, make a tentative outline of the first choices for staff positions. (See Form ST-1 in Appendix A.) Place your strongest people in the areas of greatest responsibility. Get an overview of your camp. As you make personal contact with prospective workers, give them copies of the appropriate staff position material from this manual.

The Camp Director must also design a set of procedures and safety rules for the camp week as well as be responsible for advising the staff of them. A sample list is provided.

Daily Dismissal Procedures
At the end of the day, have the campers sit in the auditorium with their assigned groups. All campers should return their name tags and pick up their empty lunch boxes. Parents and guardians come into the back of the auditorium to wait. One by one, parents call the name or names of their campers. These children immediately go to the parent/guardian, receive a newsletter, and walk out the door. Parents and campers are encouraged to leave the building together, quickly, to eliminate any confusion.

There should be no unattended children loitering around the church or parking lot. This dismissal procedure takes a little longer, but we have found that the parents are appreciative of the effort to protect their children rather than being frustrated over the time involved. Parking lots can be very dangerous. One hundred children running wildly out of a building into a parking lot is an accident waiting to happen!
After a performance, children remain on stage while the

Director and Group Leaders join them. Parents are asked to come to the stage and receive their children. Ask parents to keep their children with them at all times for the remainder of the evening.

Musical Director
The Musical Director can be a different person than the Camp Director, but both must work very closely together. Many decisions will be joint ones. The Musical Director is in charge of, and responsible for, the following:
- choosing the musical
- securing an accompanist
- decisions about ordering books and practice tapes/CDs (with Camp Director)
- decisions about ordering T-shirts (with Camp Director)
- working with stage and costume personnel
- cast auditions for the musical
- casting decisions
- extra rehearsals
- choreography
- whatever else needs to be done concerning the musical, rehearsals, and presentation(s)

Any of these areas that can, should, be delegated. Others will simply require your individual attention or a decision made with the Camp Director.

Registration Director/ Camp Secretary
Reminder: a "/" indicates positions that can be combinations or separate.

Our church secretarial staff is

SURVIVAL TIP

The registration staff members are the first people the campers and parents meet as the camp begins. They need to greet everyone in a happy and friendly manner.

All staff positions are important.

extremely helpful during camp preparations. They assist us in
- typing and preparing the different mailings
- registering children and receiving registration money
- keeping records
- correspondence
- making audition and special rehearsal appointments
- organizational procedures
- being the major source of information for people inquiring about the week

It is best to check early with your pastor to have an understanding about extra assistance from the church secretaries. If your church does not have a full-time secretary, or job time will not allow for extra responsibilities, recruit someone to be Camp Secretary and help with all of the above areas.

The Registration Director is very important to the camp and does not have to be a musical person. He or she does need to have the gift of organization. The Registration Director needs to be present for the entire week, but the registration assistants can be part-time workers.

The Registration Director
- takes the information that the secretary receives and prepares it for camp (See Forms PE-4 and PE-5 in Appendix A.)
- sets up a registration table on Sundays and Wednesdays at church during the month prior to camp to enlist campers
- works with the Camp Director to determine schol-

arship needs and distribution
- divides the campers into teams and should be made aware of unique problems and any high energy level children
- deals with any special needs or requests of the parents
- is in charge of registering new campers the first two mornings of camp week
- organizes the distribution of the T-shirts
- develops the special awards given at the close of the day with the Camp Director's help
- oversees the sale of T-shirts, videos, and pictures at each presentation
- provides the color-coded baskets and large totes to handle lunches
- is in charge of the animal team posters, used to help organize the week

My Registration Director always asks, "What's next on the list?" She receives few pats on the back but plays a major role in the organization and success of our camp. The registration staff members are the first people the campers and parents meet when they arrive on Monday morning. They need to be a happy, friendly staff! Visitors will have a lasting impression of your church based on the attitude and spirit of these workers. Choose this team wisely!

Finance Director
If possible, it is wise to have the church's financial secretary or a designated camp

staffer keep up with all expenditures. This individual will be responsible for:
- working with the Camp Director, music minister, or other church personnel to make sure that all financial matters follow the rules of the church
- handling all music camp receipts
- working with the Registration Director concerning camper fees
- providing petty cash to purchase supplies during the week

One year, there were some major events in our music ministry before camp began. In the high pace of those days, some of the music event expenditures were accidentally charged to the music camp account. Although it is tempting to combine many of the camp expenses into a miscellaneous column, make sure every receipt is marked to indicate an area of the camp budget such as costuming, registration, kitchen, etc. This will provide a more accurate record of finances and safeguard against mishandled or misplaced funds. In addition, there will be a clearer picture of your expenses as you evaluate for the next year.

Group Leaders
It is obvious that the Group Leaders play a very important role in music camp. A Group Leader needs to love children, show patience, wear a big smile, and be enthusiastic. If

you have enough workers, it is wonderful to have both an adult and a youth group leader for each team. Group leaders need to

- really get to know their campers
- greet their children every morning
- participate in Early Bird activities (sitting with campers, playing the games, singing the songs)
- cheer their team to victory, helping and encouraging them to win the Spirit Stick which is a special award given to the team with the best attitude
- constantly remind the campers of good behavior and positive character qualities
- go to the classes with their groups as well as learn the songs and choreography
- help individual children who are having problems with choreography or words
- know where their campers are at all times
- escort the children everywhere

When a Group Leader is in class with a teacher, the teacher is the leader in the class and a Group Leader should not interrupt the teacher. If a child is creating a problem, the group leader can quietly take the child out in the hall to talk to him or her.

- keep attitudes in check, make the schedule run smoothly, and chaperone the children in each unique activity
- should carry a black marker to write a child's name or initials on a piece of clothing, bag lunch, etc., that is not otherwise labeled
  It is very important that the camp T-shirt have the child's name on the tag.
- help their team members keep up with their belongings
  A pencil and small note pad is helpful.
- can make up a team cheer to build spirit in their group, or suggest special handshakes
- help to keep the noise level down at the appropriate times
- collect name tags at the end

of the day and return lunch boxes

- need to learn the children's names quickly
  Children love to hear their names
- can help their group with Bible quiz questions when there are a few minutes of spare time
- may have to deal with more disturbances than the other staff
  Encourage leaders to bring a child to the Camp Director for major problems. If there are unique problems, Group Leaders may need to mention these during the staff meetings in the mornings.
- must be flexible
  There are very few camps that have not needed changes during the week.
- encourage those who are shy or tenuous to participate
- should monitor bathroom breaks
  Assigning groups to specific bathrooms, or times, is very helpful.

ABC
STEPS TO BECOMING A CHRISTIAN

ADMIT to God that you are a sinner. *(Romans 3:23; Romans 6:23)*. Repent, turning away from your sin *(Acts 3:19; 1John 1:9)*.

BELIEVE that Jesus is God's Son and accept God's gift of forgiveness from sin *(Romans 5:8; Acts 4:12; John 3:16; John 14:6; Ephesians 2:8-9; John 1:11-13)*.

CONFESS your faith in Jesus Christ as Savior and Lord *(Romans 10:9-10, 13)*.

• Maintain the schedule and always wear a watch.

Lunch Responsibilities
• During the morning mass rehearsal, the youth Group Leaders take the color-coded buckets to the lunchroom and set the lunches on their team's table. After lunch the campers put their lunch boxes back in the buckets. The youth Group Leaders are then in charge of getting the buckets back to the front area for collection at the end of the day.
• Adult Group Leaders need to sit with their teams during lunch. They should remind campers to talk quietly, as well as help with clean up, etc. This will maintain a more controlled lunch time.

Presentation Responsibilities
• During the performance of the musical, several Group Leaders sit on the sides of the stage to help in case of an emergency. If a child falls or faints, a Group Leader is very close to help quickly, with minimal distractions. It is also a good idea to have a trash can close yo the stage if a child gets sick.
• Before a presentation, Group Leaders need to help organize their team, making sure each child is ready, and that all have gone to the bathroom.
• On Sunday night, Group Leaders introduce the campers in their group and give each a camp picture/certificate. (Group Leaders personally sign each certificate

before the presentation.) It is always nice if the leaders have something special to say about their group, such as winning the Spirit Stick or having a great attitude. If a group has an adult leader and a youth leader, the adult calls the children's names and the youth hands out the certificates.

Group Leaders must check their certificates before announcing any names to see that every child has one, and that there are no certificates belonging to children in other groups. It is a great disappointment to a child for everyone in the group to be recognized except her, simply because the leader was not thorough. To save time, Group Leaders should call only the names of the children who are present.

Carnival Responsibilities
During the carnival, Group Leaders pass out the small paper sacks to each of their campers. (The sacks should already be labeled with the children's names.) A colored dot on the sack helps the children get the sacks into their colored group buckets after the carnival. The sacks will then be distributed to the campers at the end of the day.

Most importantly, Group Leaders need to be alert. If a child wants to talk to someone about becoming a Christian, it will probably be his/her Group Leader. Every Group Leader

SURVIVAL TIP
Group Leaders need to be alert. If a child wants to talk to someone about becoming a Christian, it will probably be his/her Group Leader. Every Group Leader needs to be able to share the plan of salvation.

needs to be able to share the plan of salvation.

Music Teacher

A musical person is usually asked to be in this position. Your selection of teachers will depend on the level of musical training you and/or the Musical Director want from them during the class. It helps if they have some training, but usually it is not absolutely necessary.

Most musicals have supplementary material that gives ideas for teaching the songs, such as activities, worksheets, theory, games, etc. This can be very helpful for the teacher, eliminate a great deal of work, and add some real sparkle to the music classes. The Musical Director should have and provide these resources.

A Music Teacher
• is given one or two songs
• should teach the songs and the choreography
• needs to be alert to the following problems when learning and teaching choreography
(1) If facing the children when teaching the motions, the children should be able to mirror the teacher and do the motions correctly. In other words, the teacher must do the motions opposite or backward when facing the children.
(2) If your back is toward the children, this may be easier and everyone does the movements the same.
(3) The confusion happens

when the Music Teacher varies her position by sometimes facing the children and sometimes having her back to them. My suggestion is to do it the same every time. If not, you are going to have a room of confused campers.
• will set up the rooms during the Early Bird activities so that everything is ready to begin when the children transfer to classes
Rooms should be set up to allow easy flow of campers to their seats.
• will be sure recordings are cued so there is no delay in getting started
• will help with costumes, scenery, or other tasks when not teaching

If the musical recordings were sent out early, most of the children will partially know the music. We spend only two days in music classes, so it is very important that the Music Teacher use this time wisely.

Drama/Choreography Coordinator

This person will act as the Musical Director's assistant and can also be on the camp staff as a Music Teacher. This person's responsibilities include the following:
• sitting beside the Musical Director during the mass rehearsals to maintain a running list of things that need to be done, props or ideas that come to mind, errands, notes for the director, etc.
• being a prompter for the speaking parts

• working with the Musical Director to determine choreography, remembering that motions need to be natural for the children
For example, most children use their right arm/foot more easily.
• teaching the choreography to the Music Teachers
• alerting the Music Teachers to the following problems when learning and teaching choreography:
(1) If facing the children when teaching the motions, the children should be able to mirror the teacher and do the motions correctly. In other words, the teacher must do the motions opposite or backward when facing the children.
(2) If your back is toward the children, this may be easier and everyone does the movements the same.
(3) The confusion happens when the teacher varies her position by sometimes facing the children and sometimes having her back to them. My suggestion is to do it the same every time. If not, you are going to have a room of confused campers.
• organizing large paper sacks for each child with name on the outside and special costume on the inside, if special costuming is required

Accompanist

This person could also act as the Musical Director's assistant if necessary. The position could be filled by the church organist or pianist, by a Music Teacher who plays piano, or even the Musical Director. An accompanist may only be needed for mass rehearsals early in the week unless the Musical Director has chosen not to use an accompaniment track.

Early Bird/Opening Assembly Coordinator

Every morning, from 8:40 a.m. (sometimes earlier) until 9:00 a.m., we have Early Bird activities. Regardless of the schedule, this segment starts approximately 20 minutes before the official day begins, or when there are early arrivers. Unattended children should not be wandering the building. Remember, your staff children can be in a separate room doing their own activities until Early Bird time begins. (See Child Care Coordinator section in this chapter.)

Some camps prefer to have an Opening Assembly that is the first 20 minutes of camp. This time can be basically the same each morning and also gives the latecomers a little more time. The leader(s) for this time must have energy and enthusiasm. Their job is to get the children awake and ready for the day's events. They also encourage and help build team spirit among the groups. This time involves a variety of activities including recreation-

SAMPLE DAILY LESSON PLAN

8:35-8:45 a.m. Start with something simple
- warm-up songs, vocalises
- stretch and movement activities
- body energizers

8:45-8:50 a.m. Choruses or Simple Team Builders
Choose songs that will get children up and moving. Choose games that require participants from each of the teams. Team builders should be designed to build team spirit. Encourage the older children to help the younger ones. Don't worry whether the teams always have the same number of children present. If a game depends on numbers, add a youth worker or team leader. Encourage team members to cheer loudly for their team mates.

8:50-9:00 a.m Chorus
Sing "cool down" songs with the children.
Our main schedule begins at 9:00 with a quick time of instruction from the Camp Director and a short character lesson. Individual classes begin at 9:10. Starting classes on time is important to a well-run schedule. Favorite games can be finished or replayed at recreation time.

al songs, praise and worship, skits, and simple games. We use penny candy to reward the winners. It is best not to use chocolate but a giant sack of hard candy or fruit chews work well and could last all week.

In planning your week, begin on Monday with one or two fun songs, something that is familiar and has movement. Use a "get to know you game" and a "cool down chorus." Keep it simple, but always have more planned than needed. The pace must be quick and move swiftly from one song or game to another. By

Friday, the campers can choose their favorite songs and activities from the week. Finally, the Early Bird/ Opening Assembly Coordinator needs to be ready at any time to take over and lead the kids in a game or a song at a moment's notice. Situations can arise and a director may need to slip out for several minutes or just need a break. There is never a dead time in our camp because our coordinator always has several ideas in his pocket that spell F-U-N!

Following is a very short list of choruses that will work well during the Early Bird or

Opening Assembly time. Following that are two valuable resources for other praise and Scripture songs as well as fun activity songs for use throughout the music camp week. For more information on resources and leadership aids, see Appendix D. Ideas for games and team builders are included in the Recreation Coordinator's job description which follows this one.

Sample Choruses
- "Hallelu, Hallelujah, Praise Ye the Lord"
- "The Joy of the Lord is My Strength"
- "Love Him, Love Him"
- "I Am a C-H-R-I-S-T-I-A-N"
- "Father Abraham"
- "Rise and Shine"
- "Deep and Wide"
- "I've Got the Joy...Down in My Heart"
- "The B-I-B-L-E"
- "This Little Light of Mine"

Song Resources
- *Fun & Praise*, compiled by Anita Wagoner, is filled with energy boosters and body movers for children of all ages. This collection has 20 timeless unison and 2-part songs such as: *Wah-da-lee-a-cha; My Bonnie; An Austrian Went Yodeling; Singing Skills and Motor Skills; I'm Gonna Praise Him.*
  Fun & Praise is published by Dovetail Music
- *Isn't That the Truth* is another publication of Dovetail Music and is a collection of exciting Scripture memory songs for children.

What a wonderful way for children to hide God's Word in their hearts. Titles include: *The New Testament Song; No Other Name but Jesus; Salvation: Romans 3:23; Give Thanks to the Lord.*
Both of these collections are also available on cassettes and CDs.

Recreation Coordinator and Leaders
The Recreation Coordinator position, as with many others, is optional. If the camp is structured in such a way that the afternoons are filled with recreational-type activities, then this staff person could coordinate all of that. If the camp schedule has a specific recreation class or time built in, the play can be organized or non-structured. Free play on the church playground or gymnasium would be ideal for some with the Recreation Coordinator and Leaders there to supervise. Others may prefer structured play in the form of games and team building exercises led by the recreation staff. As emphasized before, develop the schedule to fit the needs and desires of your situation.

Games and Activities
These are winners, and more ideas can be found in Play It *and* Play It Again, *Edited by Wayne Rice and Mike Yaconelli, Youth Specialties, Inc., Zondervan Publishing House.*

MARSHMALLOW ON A STRING—Volunteer Game
(Five minutes)

Materials
- One 2-foot length of string per team
- One marshmallow per team

Preparation
Tie one marshmallow to the end of each string.

Playing Instructions
- Ask for two volunteers from each team.
- Volunteer 1 puts the string with the marshmallow tied to the end of it in his/her mouth.
- Position Volunteer 2 next to Volunteer 1 with hands behind own back.
- Without using hands, Volunteer 1 will swing the marshmallow string back and forth while Volunteer 2 attempts to catch the marshmallow in his/her mouth.
- The first team to successfully catch the marshmallow and eat it, wins.

●●●

VASELINE® AND COTTON BALL RELAY
(Five minutes)

Materials
- Petroleum jelly
- 1 paper plate per team
- 1 plastic cup per team
- 6 cotton balls per team

Preparation
- Put a large dab of petroleum jelly on each paper plate and

space plates out in a straight line on the floor.

•Place each cup approximately 8-10 feet away from each paper plate.

•Place 6 cotton balls next to the paper plates.

Playing Instructions
Ask for six volunteers from each team. When you say, "Go!" without using hands, each contestant will dab their nose in petroleum jelly and attempt to stick one cotton ball to his/her nose. Then the contestant runs to the opposite cup and, without using hands, drops the cotton ball into the cup and runs back to starting position. The first team to complete the relay, wins.

•••

TOILET PAPER THE GROUP LEADER CONTEST (Five minutes)

Materials
1 toilet paper roll per team.

Instructions
Ask a Group Leader from each team to come to the front. Next, ask for two volunteers from each team. When you say, "Go!" the volunteers should wrap their leader with toilet paper. The first team to run out of toilet paper, wins.

•••

FUN WITH BALLOONS
(One Early Bird session during the week can be games that use balloons.)

Materials
50 Balloons

Preparation
Blow up balloons needed

Ideas for Play
• Ask for a volunteer from each team to blow up and tie a balloon. The first volunteer to succeed, wins.

•Two volunteers from each team stand back-to-back, grab arms and hold a balloon between their backs. Next, have each pair race from one point to another. The first pair to the finish line wins.

•Ask a volunteer from each team to hold a balloon with his/her knees and race from one point to the next. The first contestant to the finish line wins.

•Ask one volunteer from each team to pop the balloon by sitting on it. The first to pop the balloon wins.

•••

DRESS-UP RELAY
(Five minutes)

Materials
•5 different clothing items per team (i.e. oversized pants, old shirt, large shoes, hat, tie)

Preparation
•Divide the clothing into piles, 1 pile per team.

Playing Instructions
•Ask for five volunteers and one Group Leader from each team. The leader will stand by the pile of clothes.

•When you say, "Go!" one of the teammates will run to the leader, choose an item of clothing, put it on the leader, and then run back to the starting point to tag the next person in line.

•The first team to completely dress the group leader, wins.

•••

PASS-IT-ON RELAY—Team Building Game (10 minutes)

Materials
•straws or tennis balls for each team

Preparation
•Set up a straight row of chairs for each team, one chair for each team member, three or more feet between rows.

Playing Instructions
•Team members take off shoes and socks. (Make sure socks are put inside shoes and each team has all shoes/socks together in their team bucket.)

•Each team sits in a straight row of chairs and the child on the end (captain) begins to pass a straw or tennis ball to the next person, using only his feet or toes, no hands allowed.

•The second child takes the straw or tennis ball with her feet or toes and passes it on in like manner.

•The captain continues to send more straws down the line.

•The object of the game is to pass as many straws or tennis

balls to the end of the line in the appointed time period as possible.

●●●

LAST ONE STANDING GAME *(Five minutes)*

Materials
- List of descriptions for questions
  ○ your first name starts with a P
  ○ you have a birthday in June
  ○ you have red hair
  ○ you have on white tennis shoes
  ○ you did not brush your teeth today
  ○ you are wearing a pink shirt
  ○ your toothbrush is blue
  ○ you have on jewelry
  ○ you have been to Music Camp for three years
  ○ you are wearing jeans
  ○ you have lived in (City/Town) all of your life
  ○ you don't like spinach
  ○ you were in the Yellow Yaks last year
  ○ you have on anything blue
  ○ you are not wearing socks
  ○ you had a peanut butter sandwich yesterday
  ○ you have been to a professional baseball game this year
  ○ you have a younger sister
  ○ you have eaten at (name of a favorite fast food eatery) this week
  ○ you are a staff child
  ○ you will turn 10 this month
  ○ you have ever sung a solo
  ○ you have on a watch
  ○ you wear glasses
  ○ you have colored shoe laces
  ○ you have on a WWJD bracelet
  ○ your clothing has pockets

Playing Instructions
- All the children stand.
- As you begin to ask the questions, the children sit if the question is true for them. (Obviously, you can change this list to fit your situation.)
- The last child standing is the winner, as well as his team.

●●●

HUMAN SCAVENGER HUNT *(5-10 minutes)*

Materials
- a list of items such as: wallet, glasses, hair ribbon, hole in the sock, toe nails painted, a cross necklace, overalls, two shirts, piece of string, rubber band, head band, comb, penny, nickel, dime, quarter, dollar bill, a hat, ring, belt, ponytail holder, etc.

Playing Instructions
- The leader stands in the center of all the children.
- When she calls out one of the items, the first child to go up and show the leader the item, wins a point for their team.

●●●

SIMON SAYS
Play like the traditional game.

●●●

1 TO 30?—Team building Game *(10 minutes)*

Materials
- 200 paper plates
- large black felt-tip marker

Preparation
- Each team needs 30 paper plates with large consecutive numbers 1-30 written on them, one number per plate.
- Set up the plates in a small circle, but not in order.

Playing Instructions
- Each team forms a circle around their set of plates.
- The child closest to the number 1 jumps on the plate and then jumps back. Another child then jumps on 2 and jumps back to his place.
- Different children are jumping on the consecutive numbers until they have jumped on all 30.
- No child can jump on the next number until the child before him is back in his place. This is designed to build team work. Let the children practice several times, and then see which group can do it the fastest. Have all children raise their hands when they have made it. Actual time is not important; however, keep a count of who wins each game and award a prize at the end for the most wins.
- After playing several times, ask the children to move to a new place around the circle and start again.

●●●

BALL TOSS

Materials
beach ball

Playing Instructions
- Throwing the ball out into

the crowd of children can be great fun. Count and see how many times the children can hit it in the air before it touches the ground. By the end of the week, they can really keep it going.

Bible Quiz Leader

This position is optional, but needs to be filled by a gifted teacher. It is very important that the Bible Quiz Leader
- learn the procedures of the Bible quizzing game
- adjust the game to fit the particular camp and group of children
- create original quiz questions to emphasize the scriptural basis of the musical
- read the pages describing Bible quizzing specifics from Chapter 3 of this manual

Activity/Craft Leaders

The primary requirement for this position is a willingness to, and love for, work with children. If your camp has an activity/craft class, these leaders will be responsible for:
- gathering and/or purchasing necessary supplies
- obtaining craft ideas from resources that may be provided with the musical (See the Dovetailor®, p. 139.), Sunday School teachers, or area Christian bookstores
- set up and clean up of the room and materials used

These leaders would not have to stay all day and could be people who only help on a part-time basis. Once again, this depends on the schedule

chosen, one that best suits your unique situation and the focus of your ministry.

Prop and Staging Manager

This person needs to be able to spend extra hours during the week, for they are not always able to be on stage working while the campers are there.

It is nice when this person
- has no fear
- is confident of making any necessary stage design
- is not afraid of hard work or long hours
- does it all with a smile

This individual should also
- be creative and know how to make a verbal or written idea come to life
- work with the Musical Director and both come to an agreement on the message and the focus of the stage
- be advised of an estimate of the budget provided
- be given or make a list of props that will be needed for the presentation, as early as possible, which will allow time to find or create the needed items
- read the section in Chapter 5 of this manual concerning stage plans

A Word of Caution:

Anytime a special prop, special effect, or unique stage lighting, or costume is used, make sure this part is practiced with the children, and has been done successfully, several times. Do not take the chance

of something failing because it hasn't been thoroughly practiced.

Kitchen Coordinator and Aides

The Kitchen Coordinator is a vital part of any camp. It is definitely not the easiest job, but what would camp be without the goodies? The character qualities for the kitchen staff are organization, flexibility, and patience. Make the kitchen staff feel like they are a real part of music camp. It is easy to get lost in the kitchen and not be a part of the fun of preparing the musical and other special events.

The following supply list is based on 100 campers served morning snack, lunch, and an afternoon snow cone. Adjust the list according to your particular needs. Most items are purchased the week before camp begins.

Basic Supplies
- cookies—30 pkgs for morning snack
- sugar—12 to 15 4-lb. bags
- Kool-Aid®—50 pkgs. (not pre-mixed) for morning snacks and lunch
  ○ *Snack time:* 4–5 gal. of Kool-Aid®
  ○ *Lunch time:* 2 gal. of Kool-Aid®
- 2 gal. ice water
  We make our own drink because the Kitchen Coordinator feels it is much cheaper; however, it is more work. We make it the day before and cool it all night.

- plastic spoons—1 case of 1,000 for snow cones
- 6 oz. cups—4 cases of 500 cups for morning snack, lunch, and snow cones
- snow cone syrup—8 gal.
- 20 bags of ice
- napkins—1 case
- soda—16 cases for teachers only
- snow cones
  We make our own. We are blessed to have a snow cone machine at our church. These machines can also be rented.
    - 15 pkgs. pink lemonade
    - 5 cups sugar
    - 5 cups water to start
      Bring to boil and let cool. If you want it to be a heavy syrup, use less water.

Every afternoon the kitchen staff makes the ice in the kitchen and fills small foam cups (rather than paper cones) with ice and stacks them in coolers. Each cooler holds about 70 cups. Enough cups are filled to serve both the children and the adults. Minutes before the children are dismissed from their last class, the kitchen staff pours the syrup on the ice. We do not offer a choice of flavors; this produces less confusion. If a snow cone is not possible, a single Popsicle® could be just as refreshing.

Breakfast
Breakfast is only for camp staff and their children. This is another optional area; however, we have found this to be a real help to those staffers with children. The following items are suggestions for camp breakfast:
- chocolate or white milk
- doughnuts and pastries
- bagels and cream cheese
- fruit
- small cans of juice (mixed flavors)

In our camp, the Kitchen Coordinator buys the soda and breakfast for the teachers, but the other food and snacks for the teachers' Staff Retreat Room fall under a separate staff person's responsibility. Although these two areas could be combined, it makes both jobs difficult for one person. Maybe a Kitchen Aide could be given this responsibility.

Lunch
Cost for lunch can be as high as $700-$1000. Having children bring a sack lunch is much less expensive. However, simple menus and buying food in bulk can provide a delicious week of lunches for the campers.

Suggestions:
Nachos, lemonade, bite-sized candy bars
- 5-6 gal. cheese sauce
- 4 lg. boxes bulk chips
- 1 gal. Jalapeño peppers
- 2 gal. chili w/out beans

Grilled hamburgers, cheeseburgers, or hot dogs; chips; lemonade; small candy bars
- 5 boxes of 40 pre-formed patties
- 160 cheese slices

SURVIVAL TIP

Parents providing a sack lunch will eliminate problems: expense of preparing and serving a meal, picky eaters, and food allergies.

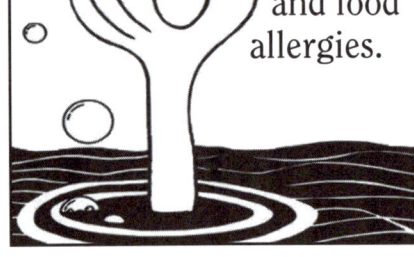

- 25 pkgs. hot dogs
- 25 pkgs. buns
- Condiments (mustard, ketchup, mayo, relish)

Other ideas:
Pizza
Subs from a sub shop
Chicken strips
Corn dogs
Sandwiches
Tacos

Staff Retreat Room

Sometimes, the only place of quiet refuge during camp is found in the Staff Retreat Room. It can be a room where the camp staff can get away for a cold soda, coffee, or refreshments. If necessary, it can be the kitchen with the door shut. The staff breakfast is also provided here. Our Coordinator, Aides, and the women of our church go the extra mile and often bring in lunch items and special treats. It really is a fun place of fellowship. The camp staff becomes quite close that week because we have had some time to fellowship every day.

It is nice to have one person whose only responsibility is to take care of this room. If she has other responsibilities, it can often be too much. This individual becomes everyone's favorite person because she has the coffee ready bright and early every morning.

Reception Coordinator

The Reception Coordinator should be someone with the gift of hospitality who knows how to create a wonderful atmosphere for fellowship. A reception after the musical presentation can be another opportunity for witnessing, introducing others to the church, and fellowship. During the entire week of camp, the kids have made themselves at home. Many of the visiting parents, however, have only stepped inside the door. They have watched their children perform, but they have not really fellowshipped with, or gotten to know, the camp staff. It is with this thought that we have planned the reception. Our camp staff, deacons, and church family are alerted to the mission for Sunday night—to minister to the campers' parents. It is our prayer that these parents will feel at home and have the freedom to call on the church if they ever have a need.

The Reception Coordinator must do the following:
- Contact a bakery, giving them notice that you will be ordering for a particular evening. Ask for the last date that an order can be placed. By Tuesday of camp week, you should know the approximate number of campers and can estimate the reception attendance. A reasonable estimate would be between two and three times camp enrollment.
- Decide on refreshments.
  - two full sheet cakes will serve about 100 people.
  - cookies—25 dozen per 100 (Rule of thumb: most people take three cookies.)
  - punch—5 gal will serve 100 6-oz servings
- enlist servers—2 to serve punch; 3-6 to serve cake and cookies and replenish table(s) and 4 additional helpers to clean up
  Try to choose people for the reception that have not worked during camp.
- work with the Kitchen Coordinator to purchase napkins, cups, and eating utensils
  These supplies are not included on the kitchen director's supply list.
- decide on tablecloths, centerpieces, and other decorations
  The theme of your reception should be an extension of your musical.

Carnival Coordinator

If you choose to have a carnival, try to find one or two people to take over the planning of it. We have people who are unable to help for the entire week, but may be able to take off one or two days from work. The carnival is a perfect time for this extra help. A husband and wife team is also a nice way to coordinate the carnival.

The Carnival Coordinator is responsible for:
- making sure the carnival is ready to go at the time it's scheduled
- setup, which takes place during a mass rehearsal so that most of the camp staff is available to help
- working with the Camp Director to order prizes
- dividing prizes into plastic

bags or baskets for each game
The prizes are for simply playing the game. Everybody wins!
- making sure all games and activities are supervised
- working with the Kitchen Coordinator to purchase food and refreshments
- working with the kitchen staff to transport and set up food and drinks at the carnival

Food for Carnival Day
- 10–15 gallons of ice water
- 10–15 gallons of Kool-Aid®
- Snow Cones
  ○ 15 pkgs. pink lemonade
  ○ 5 cups of sugar
  ○ 5 cups of water (If you want heavy syrup, use less water.)
- Popcorn is popped for the carnival. We prepare one bag per child and per adult at the camp. We fill the bags in the kitchen and carry them outside.
- Hot Dogs (1 per person)
  ○ 25 packages of hot dogs (Watch expiration dates on packages.)
  ○ 25 packages of buns
  ○ 2 large squeeze bottles of Mustard
  ○ 2 bottles of Ketchup
  If you have a person in your church that loves to grill, ask him to bring a grill and start cooking early in the day. Remember, it takes a lot of time to grill over 200 hot dogs. This year, we decided to have the carnival after lunch and did not serve hot dogs. We liked that schedule, and it did cut down on the cost.

- Cotton Candy
  Rent a cotton candy machine. Children love cotton candy and it makes for great fun. Be aware that a deposit may be required to reserve the machine. Call early and check the policy. Cotton candy supplies are usually available at the rental store as well.

More details about carnival preparation can be found in Chapter 3.

Child Care Coordinator and Workers

As you recruit staff for your entire camp, determine the number of nursery and preschool children that will need child care.
The Camp Director, Child Care Coordinator, and Workers need to be aware of the following:
- Compliance with the state requirements for the ratio of children to caregiver must be met.
- Realize that these are long days for the little children and their caregivers. Because of this, we pay our child care workers. It adds to the expense of the camp, but it is very necessary to obtain enough staff.
- These children can be included in as many camp activities as possible (e.g. carnival or other fun outdoor time, camp picture and camp video, etc.).
- A small child's pool with very little water, or a sprinkler, can be used outside during the afternoon for refreshing

water play. Sometimes these children can go into the auditorium and watch the musical rehearsals for short periods of time.
- Parents should bring an extra pair of clothes each day, and a pillow.
- All bring a sack lunch and have a picnic outside or in the room.
- It is important that these workers get breaks during the day. Sometimes a volunteer can spend some time with the little ones during lunch so the workers can take a break.
- Child care hours should be posted for everyone to see.

Staff Children's Room

Because our staff is asked to be in a meeting at 8:00 a.m., the camper children of the staff need to be cared for during this time. Any children who come to camp with an adult staff person are considered staff children.

There is usually one adult worker in this room with two youth workers. (It is best not to use Teacher or a Group Leader.) Stock the room with a VCR, Bible videos, board games, crayons and paper, etc., for these children.

They are served breakfast at 8:00 a.m. At 8:40, these children are dismissed to the auditorium for Early Bird activities. At the close of the day, or before closing assembly, each Group Leader begins to collect name tags and return lunch boxes. Staff children are dismissed to the staff children's room to await their parents. They return to the same room as in the morning, to play games, watch videos, etc. One of the main reasons we started a staff children's room was that during the parent pick-up, the camp staff children did not get picked up. It was hard to know when all the regular campers were gone and when only staff children were left.

With this special room in place, as soon as the auditorium is without children, all staff are encouraged to finish their duties quickly, collect their belongings, pick up their children, and vacate the building. The staff children's room is open until 3:30 p.m.; therefore, all staff children should be picked up by then. We encourage staff to take their children home, even if they must return later in the evening. This is done for many reasons:
- Staff who return to work on staging and costumes do not need to be supervising children as well.
- Microphones and equipment may be unattended and children running on the stage could damage them.
- Primarily, this helps prevent unattended children from getting hurt.

Camp Nurse
A camp nurse
- should have some experience and training in nursing or be an Emergency Medical

Technician (EMT)
- should have a complete first-aid kit ready when camp begins
- should be provided with a nurse's station that is in a very visible location
- should not be in a room alone with a child and always keep the door open, or have another staff person present in the room
- should be very professional

If a child is sick, call their family to come and get them. If a child does become ill and cannot return to camp, we try to give them back part of their registration fee. This will depend on when the camper stops coming and if he or she has received the book, tape, and T-shirt.

Special Guidelines for Medication and Illness
Music camp is not equipped to handle a sick child or a child that consistently feels bad. It is preferable not to give out medication, but the Camp Nurse should be available to discuss, with parents, any unique problems regarding a child and medication. A permission slip with exact information should be filled out and signed by the parent. Be sure there is an emergency phone number where a caregiver can be reached anytime, every day, of camp.

SURVIVAL TIP

The safety and security of each camper is a top priority and every leader's job. Prior detailed planning will provide a safe and secure camp for all participants.

Advertising and Publicity/ Newsletter Editor

Many times this is the Camp Director. If there is a person in your church who is gifted in publicity, allow him or her to
- create a special advertisement
- use the supplementary materials available with the musical that often have advertising helps
- discuss with the Camp Director how much money is budgeted for advertisements

Areas in which to advertise are:
- the religious section of the local newspaper
- free community calendar of events announced on radio or TV
- local Christian radio stations
- area churches
- citywide children's choirs (where available)
Ask permission to hand out flyers.
- local Christian and public schools (Get permission.)
- local Girl Scouts® and Cub Scouts®, or Awanas at area churches
The person who does a newsletter and/or the printed program for the musical performances should have computer skills. Perhaps a church secretary can assist in this area.

The Newsletter Editor will need to
- get a newsletter ready to be given to the children at the close of each camp day.
- find out daily from the Camp Director and Musical Director any messages needed for the newsletter
- secure a list of Bible quizzing questions for the following day.
- prepare the printed program for the night of the musical presentation.

It is always nice to have every child's name in the program. The children love to see their names in print, and it makes for a treasured keepsake. Double check spelling of all names from registration cards, and obtain a cast list from the Musical Director. Also, we like to print an additional sheet that recognizes each staff worker. This is one way to affirm them for all of their dedication and hard work. With 100 campers, print 300 copies of the program for each night of the presentation.

Camp Videographer/ Photographer

The camp video can include candid shots taken throughout the week. Special highlights, behind-the-scenes activities, practice sessions, and classroom shots are all caught on video. These candid shots capture the true spirit of music

---

LAKESIDE BAPTIST CHURCH

Daily Camp Journal

SUMMER WEEK OF CHOIR   **JULY 19, 2000**

Big Quiz-Off Tomorrow!

Parents are invited to the "Big Quiz-Off," which is scheduled for 1:45 - 3:00 p.m. The format is similar to "Jeopardy!" and is a fast-paced question and answer game based on scripture. Each of the contestant's chairs is linked to a buzzer which shows who stands up first to answer a question. This will be an exciting hour to wrap up the day.

Smile! You're on Candid Camera!

A professional video of Friday night's musical presentation will be available for only $15.00. You may order your copy of this special event on either Friday or Sunday night. You **must** have either cash or a check **when you order** your video.

> **Wear Your SWOC Shirts**
> ☞**Tomorrow!**🖙

Activities Are Really Heating Up at SWOC!

Children at Summer Week of Choir have been working so hard preparing for their musical presentations that relief is badly needed. A fire truck will stop at the church on Friday morning to spray the kids with water! The truck will arrive at 11:00 a.m., so this will be the last event of the week, remember, Summer Week of Choir ends at **12:00 Noon** on Friday.

Friday Is on the Way!

PPLAUSE! PPLAUSE!

Because of our Dress Rehearsal from 9:00 - 11:00 a.m., kids need to wear their costumes (SWOC T-shirt, dark pants or jeans, and shoes (no sandals) and also bring a pair of shorts and a shirt that they can get wet-*bathing suits are not allowed*. Kids need to bring towels (with their names on them) to dry off before they go home. The kids will wear their over-sized white dress shirt over their SWOC t-shirts during rehearsal.

camp and can be added to the presentation video as a special bonus. In the past, we have taken 5-second video shots of each child, which can be included on the video. You can also take a video of each team and maybe a team cheer or favorite Bible verse.

The person who will be making a video of the musical needs to be alerted to the presentation dates. You may choose to tape the opening night performance or take a video of all performances and edit them to make a wonderful memory.

Check with the publishing company of your musical concerning the copyrights and fees necessary to produce a video of the musical, especially if it is to be sold.

Every year we have hired a professional photographer to take a group picture on Wednesday. When organizing the campers and staff on stage, put the camp staff in the back row and the children in front using a variety of positions (kneeling, standing, and sitting). The Camp Director should have someone prepared to fill in waiting periods with songs or a quick game to keep everyone's attention. Also, instead of saying, "Cheese," choose a special word or phrase from the musical. This is sure to bring a smile!
Our photographer takes four or five pictures. The end result

is a black and white 8-by-10 certificate on card stock. The photographer will obtain the necessary signatures before the copies are made. This keeps people from having to individually sign all certificates.

After receiving the finished product, choose someone with excellent penmanship to write in the full name of each child. Certificates can be sorted by groups and distributed to Group Leaders for their signatures. These certificates are awarded on Sunday night after the musical.

Each group is called to the front of the stage by their Group Leader and introduced individually. This is a special time when each child is recognized and applauded as they receive their certificate. Parents and family are asked to stand when their child's name is called. By honoring the child, you also honor the parents. The congregation is encouraged to applaud each child for their hard work. The extra time spent applauding each child is well spent and well deserved.

Janitor
"Where there are no oxen, the feed-trough is empty, but an abundant harvest [comes] through the strength of an ox" (Proverbs 14:4).
As a mother of seven, I understand that our trough (home) is almost never empty, and sometimes unkempt. However,

the result of a home filled with oxen (children) is that there is an abundant harvest of love, laughter, joy, and strength. So it is with a church being blessed with 100 campers for an entire week.

The Camp Janitor should
• be prepared to face some challenges. The other staff, though, should try to be alert to areas where they can help.
• check the bathrooms every morning before camp begins to see that there are plenty of supplies.
• check to see if the air conditioning is on and cool in the areas that will be used for music camp. For instance, last year before a Sunday night presentation, I sent the children to the downstairs classrooms. Unfortunately, the air conditioning was not on. By the time I made it down to the children, they were so hot and sweaty, I felt terrible. I knew that this affected their presentation.
• check the teachers' retreat room. The teachers can, and should, pick up after themselves whenever possible.
• judge the children to see who has the cleanest table at lunch as part of the Spirit Stick competition (optional).

Remind the staff and campers to show appreciation to those who have extra have extra responsibilities because of music camp. We make sure the janitor receives a camp T-shirt and is a part of the camp picture. I like to invite our janitor to a rehearsal where he is introduced and the children give him a big thank you.

Staff Meetings

First Staff Meeting

Especially if this is your first year, you will want to have a staff meeting approximately two weeks before camp begins to give your staff an overview of the schedule, special events, and an outlook for the entire week. Make this a fun, yet informative, meeting to start building excitement and staff team spirit. This is a relaxed time for questions and explanations. Refreshments and a few decorations will enhance your meeting atmosphere.

For all practical purposes, staff assignments should have been made by the Camp Director through individual contacts before this meeting. Workers may come with an idea of what they will be doing; however, they will have many questions, especially if it is the first year of music camp or their first year to participate.

Prepare a vision statement which briefly describes the purpose or mission of the music camp ministry. Allow at least one, maybe two, hours for this meeting. If you are organized, things will move smoothly and quickly.

The following items should be discussed during this first staff meeting:

- Read the vision or mission statement for the week.
- Each staff member should be given individual responsibility sheet(s).
- Adult and Youth Group Leaders are assigned to their color-coded groups (Blue Bears, Green Giraffes, etc.) and given a list of children's names. This list will be incomplete since campers are still enrolling. It is always beneficial to let these staffers have a few minutes to talk together at some point during the meeting. They need to begin to learn the names of the children in their groups and to begin to pray for them as well.
- Distribute a sample of the daily schedule, or the entire week's schedule. (This may change as the week progresses.)
- Walk through Monday's schedule.
- Teachers should be given their classroom numbers. Each group will be assigned a classroom where they start the rotation of classes.
- Bathroom assignments can be made as well.
- Discuss the lunch schedule and any staff lunch breaks.
- A music tape and book should be given to those workers who do not have campers at home. Workers with their own children will receive one book and tape per family in the mail. Have extra books available so all staff can see a copy during the meeting.
- Choose one song from the musical and briefly teach it to

SURVIVAL TIP

Affirm the campers for their dedication and hard work by including each child's name in the printed program.

the staff with choreography.

- Discuss with the Music Teachers some of the logistics of teaching choreography. The children should be able to mirror the teacher and do the motions correctly. In other words, the teacher must do the motions opposite or backwards if facing the children.
- Announce the 8:00 a.m. staff meetings every morning for prayer time, breakfast, and special instructions. Child care and breakfast will also be provided for children of staff members.
- Discuss Early Bird activities (8:40-9:00) and the need for staff participation.
- A list of policies, safety procedures, emergency plans, dealing with parents, etc., should be discussed.
- Discuss any unique needs (props, mass sewing, cleaning etc.) where staff can help.
- Answer any questions.
- Hopefully, you have already asked for T-shirt sizes from your staff as you recruited them. If not, be sure and get everyone's size in a discreet manner.
- PRAY!

Daily Staff Meetings

I wish I could share with you everything discussed in our daily staff meetings. Each meeting takes on a current need or problem, a prayer request, or better way to focus the day. Be sure, if you have a staff meeting at 8:00 a.m., to do the following:

- Start on time!
- Be organized.
- Ask questions, listen to your staff, resolve problems.
- Remind your staff of the music camp vision.
- Be thorough, yet expedient.
- Most importantly, pray.

During the week I suggest these illustrations to help the staff focus and catch the vision:

- We have worked hard to prepare and to be organized, but if the Lord does not breathe life into this, we are but a clanging cymbal!
- "Unless the Lord builds a house, its builders labor over it in vain; unless the Lord watches over a city, the watchman stays alert in vain" (Psalm 127:1).
- What child will you influence this week for eternity?
- "As the rain and the snow come down from heaven, and do not return to it without watering the earth and making it bud and flourish, so that it yields seed for the sower and bread for the eater, so is my word that goes out from my mouth: It will not return to me empty, but will accomplish what I desire and achieve the purpose for which I sent it" (Isaiah 55:10-11, NIV).
- 2 Kings 18-19 is a wonderful passage. It looks at the struggle between King Hezekiah and the King of Assyria. During this very challenging week of music camp, there are going to be some major struggles. There will be battles

SURVIVAL TiP

Encourage your staff to see each detail of the week as an opportunity to be faithful in that which is small.

that you and the staff will face. It is important not to be deceived by the lies of the enemy. In Chapter 19, Hezekiah took the letter that was meant to cause fear, frustration, and dismay, and "Spread it out before the Lord" (2 Kings 19:14, NIV). God saw Hezekiah's heart and heard his prayer. We, as a staff, want to continually spread our battles before the Lord, seeking the victory that can only come from Him.

- "But He said to me, My grace is sufficient for you: for power is perfected in weakness...for when I am weak, then am I strong." (2 Corinthians 12:9-10). It will not be our talent, creativity, or organizational gifts that will bring true success to our week. It will be His grace and His strength.
- "Whoever is faithful in very little is also faithful in much" (Luke 16:10). Check with your local library and find a children's book about Booker T. Washington. His story is a great example of being faithful in the little things and how it affected his life.

Monday Morning:
First Day of Camp
At 8:00 a.m., the staff meeting needs to begin.
Remember to:
- Restate the Vision Statement. If the staff has not yet caught the vision of the week, they need to now!
- Remind everybody, except the Group Leaders, that they

should vote for the group that shows the best attitude, attentiveness, enthusiasm, etc., during the day. The votes need to be given to the designated person for a tally at the end of the day.
- Encourage the staff to be flexible and positive!
- Instruct that if there is a problem, bring it to the Camp Director rather than murmur and cause dissension.
- Caution all about language. Church people have high standards. During the camp, leaders must be extremely careful about their choice of words. I ask for a very high standard of conversation. When talking to a child or another adult or worker, don't use slang or inappropriate terms to describe an action or the name of something.
- Ask the youth leaders to be careful as they interact with each other. This is not a week for flirting and inappropriate behavior. They must hold a very high standard of conduct and be very mature, using self control and discretion.
- Remind everyone that their focus must be on the children. Staff behavior during this week could be discussed in 100 homes every night. It should be the staff's desire that the week would honor the Lord; and, that the church would be an example to the community.
- Answer any last-minute questions.

- Go over the policies, briefly, one more time.
- Pray for this first day and the week as a whole.
- Get ready to welcome the campers!

One Group Leader from each team should stay in the auditorium with the campers when they arrive. The other Group Leaders need to greet the campers as they leave the registration table to join the Early Bird activities.

chapter 5
PRODUCTION/ STAGING

Selecting a Musical

The spirit and message of your camp depend greatly on your musical. I begin to seriously look for a musical in January since our camp is usually in the summer. Also, many new works are released about that time.

Resources
Music Publishing Companies
•LifeWay Church Resources
1-800-436-3869
www.lifeway.com
(These children's music resources are described Appendix D.)
•Christian Music Publishers Association
www.cmpamusic.org
•Coalition of Internet Church Music Publishers
www.redshift.com/~ bowmsl/cicmp/

My recommendation is to contact companies and request a preview packet for a few of the top-selling children's musicals for the year. Most companies have preview packets of musicals available for a nominal fee. LifeWay Church Resources offers the Dovetail Club of Inner Circle, a preview of the latest releases in children's music from LifeWay Church Resources, that arrives three times a year. Some companies will even send these out for preview with no charge if sent back within a certain number of days. Be sure to ask if there are any new releases that may not be listed in catalogs or on web sites yet. There may also be videotapes available which will help you in your selection; however, you should listen to the audio recording

first and then decide about the video.

Minister of Music
Check to see if your minister of music regularly receives preview packets or is in a choral club that includes children's musicals. Your minister may also know of area church music conferences which have exhibits including children's music.

Christian Stores/Outlets
Christian stores may have demonstration recordings you can listen to in the store or check out for several days.

Area Churches
You may wish to check with other churches in the surrounding areas to see if they are doing any musicals. It is nice to attend an actual presentation. The church may allow you to borrow or rent some of their props, costumes, etc. If so, it would be considerate to give a donation to their music or drama program, which will enhance future cooperation.

Considerations
•Is the musical current? Has the musical been performed already in area churches? We have many children that come to our camp from other churches. Many of those area churches do children's musicals. We prefer to choose a work that is new, if possible, so that every child gets to experience a new and fresh message. Even an older

musical would fit this criterion if it has not already been done in your area.

•**How expensive will this musical be?**
For instance, the cost of recordings and books will vary. Some publishers sell in bulk, others do not. Bulk pack rate is usually cheaper. When you order in quantity, you can expect to receive 20%-30% off of the retail price.

•**Can our camp do this musical if only our church's children attend?**
Be sure that all speaking and singing roles can be covered as well as extras and understudies.

•**Am I selecting the right level of difficulty (unison, two or three parts) for the children involved?**
Also, consider the range of the music in relation to children's voices. Much of the music written for children today is actually too low for their best singing.

•**Who might be able to handle the lead roles and other major speaking/singing parts?**
You will possibly bring into camp new talent, but you need to be able to fill all those leads from within your church, just in case that outside talent does not show.

A word of CAUTION: Be careful of musicals that have one major lead. You must have a child that can carry the whole show. This is possible and can be a wonderful thing if you have the right child. You may want to choose a musical with more parts, so that you are not heavily dependent on a single child.

•**How many male and female parts are there?**
Sometimes these parts are interchangeable, but sometimes they are not.

•**What type of music is accepted in your church and local community?**
Some churches are more conservative than others. Does this musical fit my church? What is the message in the musical? Is it "fluff," or true seed planting?

•**Check to make sure that the musical you choose is in stock and that there is plenty of material.** This can alert you to any potential problems with ordering, shipping, or getting the order when needed.

•**Pray that God will give you wisdom.** Once you have made a preliminary decision, you may want to have several key people listen to the musical and ask their opinion. After listening to the musical a few times, you should be able to hum or sing along with the melody of the main songs. I always let my own children listen to the musicals. I can tell very quickly if it can be learned easily, or if it is very "singable." Ask the children to explain to you the message of the musical. You can learn a lot from a child's point of view.

Copyright Issues

Proverbs 3 states "Trust in the Lord with all your heart, and do not rely on your own understanding; think about Him in all your ways and he will guide you on the right paths. Don't consider yourself to be wise; fear the Lord and turn away from evil...for the Lord will be your confidence and will keep your foot from a snare" (Proverbs 3:5-7, 26). God's promises give us great motivation to do what is right. In the area of copyright laws, we are sometimes unsure what is legally okay and what is not. We have fine musicians who are writing children's musicals. To ensure the future of this type of work, these writers need to be compensated for their time and energy. At the same time, when we are on a tight budget and we learn we must pay extra to do certain things, it can discourage us very quickly, even to the point of changing our musical plans. This is NOT what the writers or the copyright laws want to accomplish. They want you to perform their work. Below are a few guidelines and suggestions that might help in this area.

•Different publishing companies have various charges and procedures. This may be something you will want to investigate **before** you select your musical. How the musical and supplementary material are used determines the pricing.

- For any type of copying, you must seek permission from the publisher and pay the royalty charge. Call the publishing company and talk with a representative that deals with copyrights.
- There may be different departments within a publishing company that will handle videos, music, recordings, television rights, etc. Check any and all of these you are considering.
- A CCLI (Christian Copyright Licensing International) license does **not** automatically give permission to copy a children's musical.
- Copyright laws are very extensive. *The Church Guide to Copyright Law*, by Richard Hammar is a resource providing information and advice about copyright laws. It is available from Christian Ministry Resources at 800-222-1840.
  Other on-line resources are
  - *www.cmpamusic.org* (Church Music Publisher's Association)
  - *www.loc.gov/copyright/* (United States Copyright Office home page)
  - *www.ccli.com* (Christian Copyright Licensing International)

Don't panic! These expenses can be absorbed in the registration fee. Our decision to purchase the books and listening recordings eliminate so much hassle in the long run.

Other Decisions

Books and Recordings

Books and practice recordings can be ordered, one for each family, and figured into the registration fee. This way, the children have most of the musical memorized before they come to camp. Also, all those with speaking roles or solos will have a book with which to memorize their parts. This book, with a recording, is valuable in that the children will be able to use it throughout the year and refresh the concepts they learned in music camp. An extra benefit is that the parents will be hearing the musical as well. Seeds can be planted in their lives, too.

Some other alternatives for ordering books and recordings include:
- Purchasing books and recordings only for the main characters
- Purchasing books and recordings only for teachers
- Purchasing only the amount of books or recordings absolutely necessary

We have found it worth the extra expense to order one recording and one book per family. It enables us to spend more time on stage and in fun activities because much of the music is already familiar and often memorized.

Order books and recordings as soon as possible. Be sure you have the approval of the appropriate personnel (music director, pastor, etc.). For a camp of 100 children, we order 75 recordings and 75 books. For a camp of 75 children, order 60 of each. For a camp of 50 children, 40 should be enough. These are only estimates. Decide what is best and most cost effective for your church and camp.

T-shirts

T-shirts have several purposes. They create unity and team spirit. They will promote and advertise your camp and your church all year long. They can also be worn as the basic costume for your presentation.

Costumes

If you will be renting costumes, making your own costumes, or having professionals make costumes, start the process early! Talk to the personnel you choose. Reserve any unique costumes, material, or special items that you will need.

Sound Equipment and Lighting

If you will need to rent this type of equipment, find someone who has a good reputation for this type of work. Do not hesitate to interview several people or companies. Do not be afraid to negotiate. Discuss your needs with them and schedule your dates and times.

A Word of Caution: Anytime a special prop, special effect, unique stage lighting, or costume is used, make sure this part is practiced with the children, and has been done successfully, several times. Do not take the chance of something failing because it hasn't been thoroughly practiced.

This equipment needs to be set up in the auditorium as early in the week as possible. Make sure it is all set before your last complete day of camp and, most certainly, dress rehearsal.

Video

If someone will be making a video of the musical, he or she needs to be alerted to the presentation dates. We prefer to video the first performance or "opening night." This year, we took a video of all 4 performances and edited them to make a wonderful memory. In the past, we have taken five-second video shots of each child, which can be edited into the video. You can also take short video footage of each team. Normally, the video equipment needs to be setup in the auditorium after the lighting and sound equipment are set. Check with your publishing company about the rights to produce a camp video that includes the musical performance.

Mass Rehearsals

Planning Backward

When I was in high school, I had the privilege of helping my choir director plan the rehearsal schedules for our spring musicals. We always started the planning, not at the beginning days of rehearsal, but on opening night. We would plan backward! I have learned that this principal works regardless of the number of days or the number of

rehearsals. In fact, when you have a five-day camp and are trying to pull a performance together in such a short time, you better have a plan and know what must be accomplished at each rehearsal. The goal is to be ready for the opening night presentation. This is important, whether you have a three-day camp, a 10-day camp, or whether you are working on a Christmas musical for several months. Form PS-8 in Appendix A is a Rehearsal Planning Sheet to help you prepare for each rehearsal.

For example, in our **Monday through Friday camp,** here is how I would plan backward.

Friday
(Remember, we dismiss at 12:00 p.m.)
- at 10:00 a.m. My goal is to have a smooth and complete dress rehearsal with lights and sound. No Stops!
- at 9:00 a.m. I have a complete dress and technical rehearsal with the sound and lighting people. Solve any problems, now! Truthfully, I would rather have the technical rehearsal on Thursday, but because we rent our sound and lighting, and for cost purposes, we have to do it at this time.

In order for this to happen on Friday, I must do the following things on Thursday.

Thursday
- We must practice how we will enter the auditorium to

begin the musical.

- Perfect the finale. Our curtain call needs to click; props, entrances, costuming changes must be worked out.
- Place the finishing touches on scenery.
- See that everything is ready for a complete run-through without sound and lighting.
- Instructions or tech books should be ready for the technical people, and there should be a walk-through for technical people only sometime before Friday morning.

In order for this to happen on Thursday, I must do these things on Wednesday.

Wednesday

- We must be able to go through the entire musical, even if all the props and details are not quite ready. It is time for the musical to begin to flow. Each scene should begin to run smoothly. Try to work out as many problems as possible. We even block the curtain call and, by the end of the day, it's in good shape.
- We try to have the stage finished by Wednesday morning so it will look nice in the camp picture.
- If your finale is unique, and you're adding "spice" to the moment, be sure you have at least blocked that scene and made the children aware of what is happening.

Tuesday

- We really begin to add the complete story line on

Tuesday. It is advantageous to run through the musical with solos and speaking parts as soon as possible. We usually do the first half of the musical in the morning and the remainder in the afternoon.

- The choreography has been learned and we are pulling that together, making sure things do not get sloppy.
- The children must learn when they can sit and when they stand in the performance. They must learn the director's signals. Also work on areas in the music that may be more difficult (e.g. dynamics, text, diction, rhythm).
- The children need to work with props if possible. They must practice to learn where a prop is picked up and what to do with it when finished. Children need to know where they can put on a costume as well as how to exit and return to the stage.
- Continue to work on choreography, trying to make it very precise.

Monday

- We place every child on stage where they are visible. As the day progresses, we make any necessary changes.
- It is our goal to do the major songs with choreography.
- Because of the extra rehearsal that I schedule for those with special parts the Saturday before camp begins, our soloists are confident and ready to step to the microphone on Monday to sing or

speak. If time permits, we will move into some of the speaking parts. If there are any leads or solos that have not been given out, make sure that any holes are filled.

- There is an explanation of staging so that children can gain a better understanding of what is taking place.
- Work on smiling, being enthusiastic, and standing still.

For this to happen on Monday, I must do some things before camp starts.

Before Camp
Friday and Saturday:

- I work with every soloist. We practice coming to the microphone and singing. We block all the scenes, especially with the children who have speaking parts. We work on expression, volume, and clarity. My goal for these children during this extra rehearsal is that they feel so confident about their part, that they can walk into camp Monday morning ready to perform in front of their peers.

Stage Placement

The first year that we had 100 children, I did not realize how crowded our stage would be. I placed each team on stage during my stage class on Monday. When we had our first mass rehearsal, it was definitely "mass" children on stage. That evening, I scrambled to borrow risers. On Tuesday, my plans were delayed some because I had to rework the stage placement. We had to work a little harder and a little faster, but by Wednesday morning, we were back on schedule.

At one point, I realized I had confused some of the younger campers about where they were to stand. I stopped and made sure that everyone was standing in the correct place. Then, we played a game.

I asked all campers to eyeball their team seats in the auditorium. They were to move to the seats so quietly that I could not hear them. Also, as they moved, campers should not touch any person or make any sound. The children were to do this by the count of 20. I closed my eyes and began to count slowly; the campers began to move. "19, 20! You did it! *Brag, brag, brag.*" We then reversed the game. As I counted this time, everyone would move back to the correct positions on stage. I would watch to see if there was any confusion about where they were supposed to stand.

We played this game several times that day to help the younger children, especially, know their places. This is also a good way to get the children on stage after an activity or at the beginning of a rehearsal.

There will always be challenges and changes in your schedule. Flexibility is very important to your camp and to your peace of mind. Working backward

can help you organize your plans and responsibilities into achievable segments.

Choreography

Choreography is a tool to help emphasize the message of a musical. Adding motions to a song can help children understand what they are singing. It can also help them express the thought better than they are able to without movement. Choreography adds variety and excitement which are very important to a program. However, if variety and excitement are consistently the only reason for movement, the true message of the musical may be lost or confused. These aspects must be carefully evaluated before camp begins.

The Approach
Different churches and different directors approach choreography in various ways. One group loves movement. The more movement, the more "professional" it looks. Every song must be packed with movement. Another group will view choreography as an opportunity to express the words and emotions of the musical. Still another director wants to concentrate on the precise message of the words and the beauty of the voices; therefore, choreography would only clutter and distract. Many people are somewhere in between, or they have never even given it much thought.

There are times when watching a performance or video, I have felt that I was at an aerobic exercise class or a cheerleading competition. It was very obvious that the musical had been professionally choreographed. Although exciting and impressive, it was evident by the children's faces that they were not expressing the truth in their message.

"No one [or musical] can be a slave of two masters..." (Matthew 6:24). In other words, there must be one priority. The other elements of the production must come under that priority. The message should be that priority. The adding of movement, costumes, lights, and sound should only emphasize and reinforce the message.

If the musical has a funny song, you definitely accent the song with funny movements which reinforces that message. If it is a serious song, emphasize the key words that will bring light and truth to a child's spirit. Sometimes children should just stand and sing without any movement. This also provides variety.

Planning
First, decide if you will be designing the choreography or if you will seek help from someone more experienced. Remember, the director does not have to be the expert in every area; find a person who is gifted in being expressive. Look for someone who has

some stage flair and good communication skills. Then ask him or her to express, through movement, an important line of your musical. If you like that, ask her to choreograph a song. Begin work slowly, making sure you are pleased before asking this person to choreograph the entire musical.

Helpful Hints
- Purchase and study the promotional video of your musical.
- Watch several children, youth, and adult productions. Keep a list of the movements or ideas that you like. As a young person, I can remember seeing a choir do a youth musical. As the young people sang about the cross, one set of movements was so expressive, so meaningful, that I still remember that scene after 25 years! It is that kind of choreography you want to find.
- While watching any type of performance, make mental notes of choreography, props, staging, lights, etc. Keep a notebook. These ideas might be modified for use in future productions.
- Children are still developing their coordination skills. If there are months to prepare a musical, the possibilities of choreography are much greater. With a one-week camp, keep it simple!
- Ask someone, who will be honest with you, about the decisions on choreography. My husband is quick to tell me if a motion has no reason or meaning. If it doesn't

enhance the message, find something else.
- Search for key words throughout a song. Find the emotion and movement that expresses those.
- As you brainstorm on movement, consider the body and the different moves you can make with head, shoulders, arms, hands, hip, legs, knees, or feet. Consider turning different directions, kneeling, and sitting. Also consider grouping children in different ways. This, alone, can add variety.
- If there is special emphasis on a single word, consider using campers as the letters. Anytime you can personify an innate object, such as a prop or certain part of scenery, and make it with a child's arms, legs, or face, it is usually a plus. Remember, though, that children probably cannot hold this type of pose for very long.
- It is not wise to let children make a circle or full turn while singing. This distorts the vocal sound to the audience. That type of movement is best used during non-vocal measures.
- Sometimes clapping can distract from the sound. If clapping is needed, use a two-finger clap. It will visually give the same movement with much less sound.
- A "freeze" at the end of a song is effective. Freezes work best when the music and voices end at the same time. Hold the freeze for several seconds; let the applause

begin; then, signal the children to break the freeze.
- Never let children drop or slap their arms down to their sides after an upward arm movement. A controlled return is just as important as a controlled placement. I tell my campers to pretend they are surrounded by thick chocolate syrup. As they raise their arms, they must pull their arms through the thick chocolate. This will add intensity and energy. To flip an arm up and down lacks heart and purpose. There are times for quick movements; but, they need to be choreographed carefully and full of energy.
- Movements should be done on a word or a particular syllable. The same is true when returning to an original position. This works best if the words or syllables are on a definite beat.
- Movements that go from point A to point B are most precise. Circular movements are difficult to unify with a large number of children.
- Learn and teach these important elements of hand and arm movement:
  - straight arms, not rounded
  - a relaxed flat hand (not cupped)
  - thumbs lying straight against the index finger, not sticking out
  - Palms can face out or turn in with a flat hand.
  - A jazz hand is an open hand with the fingers spread.
- Alert children to the distracting noise of feet. We have

even worn black socks on stage (no shoes) to decrease this noise. This will not work if you have a slick stage.

• Video spots or slides can add a nice touch to productions.

• Adding a prop to your choreography can be quite creative Some examples are: hats, handkerchiefs, a boat oar, streamers, rolled newspapers, flashlights, golf clubs, gloves, brooms, a shepherd's staff, pieces of cardboard made to look like Bibles or catalogs, umbrellas, books, colored dowel rods, pompoms, and paint brushes.

Almost anything you can hold in your hand can become a prop for a stage.

• Design the choreography to fit the prop. Always consider how to get one prop or 100 props on and off the stage, or at least what to do with them once the song is over.

• As leaders, we need to be very careful in our choice of movements. There is no place in a children's musical for any type of seductive attitude, regardless of the part or song. Matthew 18: 6 makes it very clear that there are grave consequences for causing a little one to stumble. The desire should be for a godly presentation as an offering to the Lord.

Directors, Beware
Whether you design your own choreography or get help in doing so, every director should be aware of the following:

• As you lead children, remember that they will mimic your level of enthusiasm, energy, and excitement.

• Be a good director. Learn to give good signals and good directions. A straight 4 conducting pattern may not be adequate to bring the excitement, energy, and movement needed in a rehearsal or performance.

• Teach your staff, in a very kind way, not to compete with the Musical Director for the campers' attention. A well meaning staff member once asked if she could make signs to hold up during the rehearsals and the presentation such as SMILE or SING LOUD. As she held up her first sign during a rehearsal, all 200 eyes immediately looked toward the sign. It took several measures to get the children to focus back to the director. Some of them never did. Needless to say, the signs were not used again.

• Remember that children tend to get lazy after choreography is learned. Review regularly to keep the motions precise.

• I do take suggestions from my staff about choreography, staging, etc. They have some great ideas. However, if they start giving opinions during a rehearsal, everyone may have a suggestion, even the children. I ask my staff to write down their ideas or share these with me at another time.

• Teach campers stage direction.
  ○ *up stage*—back of the stage
  ○ *down stage*—front of the stage

  ○ *stage right*— to actor's right
  ○ *stage left*—to actor's left

• Being still is just as important as having movement. Caution campers about scratching, flipping the hair, etc. Remind them to have an attentive attitude.

• The most important part of choreography is teaching children to have wide-open eyes, bright faces, and wholehearted singing.

Costumes

It is the director's job to look for the special talents of the people in the church that are potential staff workers. Finding the right person for costumes is very important. Sewing is not the only requirement. Creativity is a must!

In any production, costumes add real spice. There are many things to consider and many possibilities. Your choice of musical, the finances, and your costume staff will help determine the extent to which you costume the children.

• Will you ask parents to help?

• Will your camp T-shirts and dark shorts/pants be your basic costume?

• Can you afford to costume the entire cast with special vests or professional outfits?

• Will extensive costuming truly add to the message of the musical, or can it be done much simpler and still be effective?

• Will material and special

types of clothing be available at the time of your camp?

- Will you have to buy certain clothes during the winter for them to be available in the quantities that you need in the summer?

Situations

Camps can handle costumes in many ways.

- Some camps have a great costume team that can make every costume from scratch. Parents are not asked to provide anything except dark shoes or white tennis shoes. (Use Form ST-2 in Appendix A to find potential volunteers.)

- Some camps order professional costumes for the entire cast of the musical. I recommend Praise Hymn Fashions (1-800-760-0038 or *www.praisehymnfashions.com*). They do a great job and have some neat costumes.

- There are camps that ask parents to provide a basic costume. After paying a registration fee, most parents would prefer not to do this.

- Many camps use the basic camp T-shirt with dark shorts or pants as their costume. Only certain costumes are made by the costume team or ordered from a specialty shop.

- You may be able to find a church that has already done the musical. Ask to borrow or rent from them.

Where to Find Costumes
Mail-order Costume Companies

Some costume companies will rent an entire show of costumes for approximately $40.00 per costume. If you want to choose only certain costumes from a set, the price can be higher. These costumes may need to be shipped and timing can be crucial. This will also add to the expense.

You must know the campers' sizes early in the planning stage. (See Form PE-4 in Appendix A.) This is more challenging. If you choose this direction, plan for early audition and early casting. Understand, if you are working on a musical during the school year, the time schedule would not be the same as in a summer music camp. Therefore, this type of company would be very helpful.

Astrid's Costume Attic
7551 Commonwealth Avenue
Buena Park, CA 90621
994-2112
Astrid's is the largest supplier in the Los Angeles basin of children's costumes. They need an entire week to pull items and ship. If you send them the measurements of your stage with a picture of what you want, they will custom build your stage and ship it as well. Astrid Hickey is a Christian businessman that provides a great resource in this genre.

Local Costume Shops

We have found that ordering costumes is very difficult over the phone but not impossible. The costumes do not always match with a particular size. For example, small adult costumes will fit some children; yet, some of the children's costumes will not work for certain smaller campers.

By going to a costume shop, we were able to choose the preferred look and get all the accessories as part of the costume price. We found that we could negotiate the price in person much better than over the phone. We suggest you have pencil and paper ready when visiting, to write down each costume's rental cost as the salesperson quotes it to you. The salesperson may say that she will give you a child's price for all of the costumes. You need to have this price clarified whether renting a few costumes or many. Help the salesperson make these statements early in the conversation. Write it down! Once, we found that, after selecting all of our costumes, we decided not to take two of them. The salesperson, at that point, changed her quote since we did not take all the costumes. Be wise—ask the right questions and keep a record of what has been said.

One of our major concerns in renting costumes from a costume shop was that each costume with accessories had an estimated replacement cost from $100.00 to $500.00. Therefore, as the Musical Director, I took great care to watch over the safety and care of the rented costumes. Be aware that this is a part of the deal, and if something happens to those costumes, it could cost you big money!

Other places to look for costumes are vintage clothing stores, second-hand shops, thrift stores, etc. We keep our eyes open all year round at garage sales for unique items.

Borrowing

The university in our town has a costume department. They have allowed us to borrow from them in the past. When borrowing, it is thoughtful to give a donation to the church or organization from which you borrowed costumes, staging, or props. Always offer to have a costume professionally cleaned (get their permission to do it first). Return the costumes in a plastic cleaner's bag. This will help ensure your privilege to borrow again.

If you borrow or rent costumes from another church, you are responsible to replace every item that is lost or destroyed. You should replace the item with something of the same, or better, quality. Keep a record of each item that you borrow and write that down immediately for your own safety. It is best to do this **before** leaving the premises with the costumes. If you

notice a discrepancy in their list, call quickly to report it. Do not wait until after the presentation to report any differences. The reputation of the church, the staff, its people, and the reputation of the Lord can be damaged by not being conscientious in this area.

Be Creative!

Sometimes a simple prop can be used instead of a complete costume. For example, a Roman helmet, a gavel, a piece of cloth around the head or over the shoulder, etc. If you spend time and energy on any costume or accessory, be sure that it is truly visible and will make a real difference. If it does not, precious time is wasted. Small, detailed work is often lost on stage.

More Considerations

I prefer my campers to be in the musical as much as possible, even when they have a part with a unique costume. I suggest they sing as a member of the choir as long as possible. We work out the timing for them to leave stage and get dressed. After their special parts, they return to the choir in their costumes, if possible. I want to be professional, but I also want the campers to have great fun and great memories. Being off stage for most of a musical is neither. I like the children with special parts to make a special entrance; but after they have been seen, let them stay on stage. We ask those with special parts to wear lightweight T-

shirts and shorts under their costumes, when possible. This allows us to keep all the costumes in one room or area. It also allows children to add layers or remove layers without undressing. Sometimes this is not possible. Be sure to have costume staff available to help children get ready. A changing area for boys and another for girls will be needed if bathrooms are too far.

A large paper sack with each child's name on the front can be used to hold their costume, clothing, or shoes. These are only necessary for the children who have special costumes. If your entire cast has unique props and costumes, a large paper sack may be needed for every child.

Costume Storage

Storing costumes can quickly amount to lot of space. Clear plastic boxes are great for storing things. Spiders do not like plastic and it's easy to see what is inside. Hang as many costumes as possible. If others ask to borrow your costumes, props, or other materials, be sure these items are recorded and a responsible party signs for them.

SOUND AND LIGHTING

Renting Equipment

If your church's sound and/or lighting is not a professional, high-quality level, find experienced companies with quality equipment. When talking to these companies, ask for references. Ask what types of recent jobs they have done. Choose a company with a solid reputation. Most sound companies will rent a total package for your camp's performance with a set price rather than renting piece by piece. This package will usually include set-up and an operator. We have paid approximately $500.00 a year for sound and lighting. Do not be afraid to negotiate.

Even though the sound operator is not a member of your church, it is important that he be very professional in his dress and behavior while there. He will be a representative of your church in front of the parents. The company must understand this and, if it does not respond positively, move on to another. Also, everything should be set up, and ready, and on time for all rehearsals and performances. Attitude is so important. We do not want workers to have an attitude that says, "This is just a kids' event, no big deal." The presentation should be handled as professionally as possible. Do not hesitate to discuss these concerns from the beginning.

In addition, ask the sound representative to visit the church and meet with the Musical Director. A basic stage plan or drawing needs to be prepared to help give the company an idea of what will be taking place on stage.

Possible Needs

- Wireless microphones
- Headset microphones
- Omni-directional mics
- Hand-held microphones
- Does the company use diversity system microphones?
- CD players with numerical direct access
- Spotlight
- Microphone stands
- Sound board
- House speakers
- Monitors for the choir

If a child's part is very active and moves around constantly, rent cordless and/or headset microphones. Microphones on stands can be so much trouble when you have children of different sizes. The stand never seems to be the right height for each child, and it is not recommended that a child raise or lower the stand. What works well is to lay the microphone down on a piece of foam on the floor.

We usually have two solo areas. The children know to leave their choir spot early enough to pick up the microphone when they sing and place it back on the foam when finished. If you have a group of children with multiple lines, an omnidirectional microphone is very beneficial. Every child does not have to get right into the microphone to be heard. Even if you only have one regular, corded microphone, it is important that campers not be afraid of holding the microphone close to easily be heard. It is a

shame when you combine all the effort of preparing the musical with all the hard work the children have invested in learning their lines, and then have the audience not understand the words. Children's musicals usually have unique story lines. If the audience cannot hear a section of dialogue, they might miss the entire message.

A good CD player is a must. In rehearsal, it is much easier and quicker to find a song you want to rehearse on a CD player. In the director's score, simply look for the track number of the song, then enter that number on the CD player. The CD will start there. We use cassette tapes only in the music classes. We ask permission from the publishing company to make copies of single songs from the accompaniment CD onto a cassette tape only for practice in the individual classes.

Many churches have their sound system enclosed in a small booth. It is wise to have the sound board in the open auditorium for best results with a children's musical. Find out from the sound company what the power requirements are for the sound and lighting you have chosen. Assess your building with regard to the electrical and power requirements for sound and lighting. This is very important! An electrician can check the electrical sources and wire a temporary distribution, if necessary. You do not want to have an electrical blowout during the performance. Be wise, and check it out in advance.

You will need to negotiate when your sound equipment will be available. We use our church system to practice during the week. We ask the sound people to set up their equipment on Thursday evening before our Friday camp and evening performance. The sound system will need to remain in place through the Sunday night performance. It would be beneficial to have the equipment as soon as possible. Remember, though, every day that you have the equipment will cost more. Negotiate!

Lighting

Lighting is an another area of concern for your presentation. The danger about special lighting is that it can create shadows on children's faces. Children need to be seen. It is better to perform with standard auditorium lights and be seen than to use low lights and spot lights only to lose some of the faces in shadows. Children need to practice staying in the lighted areas on stage. A good rule is that lights should be set at no more than a 45-degree angle.

Choosing A Technical Team

When choosing a team of people to help with the sound and lighting, a technical booklet with directions is most helpful. It should include a description or drawing of each scene, where soloists and speaking parts will be located, what props and microphones will be used, etc.

A stage manager or cue person is one who knows the musical very well and helps direct the technical people to lighting and sound changes. He must anticipate, coordinate, and direct what needs to happen in the technical areas of sound, lighting, and special effects. This person needs to be very familiar with the speaking parts, solos, microphones, and staging. He must be someone who is very attentive and not someone who gets distracted easily or likes to visit.

A special word to those who run the lights and the sound. Lights need to come up on the soloist 2-3 seconds before a solo or special part. If you wait until the part starts, some of it will be missed. This holds true for microphones also. It is unfortunate to miss the first three to four words because the sound technician did not anticipate, and the system was not turned up in time. Again, choose people for these positions who are super alert. It helps if they know the musical. Encourage them to look ahead and anticipate each special part.

Sound

Split Tracks

With so many people using split tracks today, I was not going to cover this subject. However, I recently attended a beautiful new church with a new sound system. The sound people had never used a split track, and could not get it to work. That is when I decided to include this section in the manual.

A split track accompaniment differs from a stereo accompaniment track because it has two separate mono tracks. One track is for the accompaniment, and one is for the supporting voices (without solos). Two channels are required on the sound board; a Y-adapter should not be used. The channels must remain separate for the tracks to split. During practice, the track voices can be a great help to children as they are learning the musical. During the presentation, the sound technician will control the amount of voices and music to get a nice balance while the children are singing.

Be aware that monitors and house speakers must be controlled separately. Give more voice through the monitors for the children to hear. This adds support, gives them confidence, and encourages them sing better. During the performance, we usually do not feed track vocals through house speakers. If there is a point in the musical that needs more emphasis, more sound, more intensity, then the sound person can raise the level of voices in those speakers. Work with your levels and decide what is best for your needs. Some directors choose to subdue all track voices during performances. Others use the voices from the tape throughout the entire musical for additional sound. Whatever your decision, be sure that the track voices do not distort the vocal quality and diction clarity you want from your own choir.

Due to the large number of campers one year, we were concerned about adequate seating space for all parents, guests, and other church members for the performances. We decided to give two performances on Friday evening and two performances on Sunday evening. During the second presentation each night, we could tell that the children became very tired. Increasing the voices in the monitors and house speakers gave the children more support and helped considerably with the total sound.

I try to have as many solos as possible, even if they are not planned in the musical. If you decide to make a choir line into a solo, the voice channel for the monitors and the house speakers must be turned off completely during the solo. Return the track voice back to its original level after the solo is over.

The Unthinkable

It is always wise to think through the unthinkable—problems with the sound or lighting during a presentation. One year, on the very last word of the very last song in the musical, a circuit blew and killed the CD player, microphones, special lighting, etc. Fortunately, the auditorium lights, which had been off, were not affected and were turned on. I had alerted the children several times during the week that if we had a problem, they needed to look as if it were planned. It was apparent that this was a major problem, so I began introducing the curtain call without the background music. The children never missed a beat! Most people were not even aware that there was a problem.

I heard of a particular children's choir presentation where a fog machine began to smoke and fill the stage. The show kept right on going. This can make for lots of laughter and great memories. Have a plan; think through it. Never be afraid to stop a presentation for safety reasons. "The show must go on" is a great cliché, but when lives could be in danger, never take chances.

Presentation Videographer

If you choose to have a professional video made, this person will need to have experience in taping and video work. He needs to have professional equipment with several cameras. The video should be taped during the opening night presentation. Children seem more alert and excited during the first presentation. Also, if there are any technical problems with the first taping, there is always another opportunity. The camera sound should be hooked into the main sound system.

The videographer can also video still shots (five seconds each) of every camper and staff member. This is one of the ways to recognize and honor each individual. This is done on Friday night before the first performance. Group leaders help campers get into position for their pictures. Choose an area of the stage that will give a nice background. Parents will enjoy watching while their children have their pictures made. Instead of individual pictures, ask each team to pose or make up a cheer to perform on video.

The videographer will need music credits as well as director(s) and staff acknowledgements. He or she needs a program, a list of children's names, camp staff names, and a book cover of the musical. Videos can be sold before and after each presentation. Orders should be pre-paid. The video is encased in a plastic box for protection. The cover can be your own design or simply a program.

Please understand, Mom and Dad can bring the family camera and video the musical for their personal enjoyment without paying any copyright fee. If a director (or anyone for that matter) organizes the making and the selling of a video, copyright fees **must** be paid. This should be built into the price. Therefore, video prices can vary.

Determine a realistic pick-up date, usually between two and four weeks, which can be listed on an order form. The tapes can be picked up at the church office to eliminate shipping charges to individual homes. Orders from out of town can certainly be mailed.

One of the most important aspects of staging is that every child must be seen!

Stage Plans

Stage plans will vary with each production. Because each church is different, the Musical Director must make some major decisions about the stage.

Decisions
•Will the walls at the back of the stage be your backdrop? Will you be hanging scenery on the back wall of the stage? Will you be using the entire stage?

Using your whole stage gives wonderful room for campers to spread out. This is more impressive because it will look like you have a much larger group. There will be more room for movement and cho-

reography. Be sure you have different height levels so that children can be seen easily. If the back wall is your backdrop, you will need to determine what can practically be done on the backdrop. This can be limiting because you cannot paint the whole backstage of your church auditorium. This does not provide as much freedom as with a divider-type backdrop. On our stage, the backdrops must hang flat against the stage wall because we need all the room for children to stand.

•Will you use only part of the stage? Will you need to build a stage within your stage? Will you need to build self-standing walls, dividers, or a portable backdrop?

It is hard to decorate a very large and unusual stage. It can be helpful to section off an area, building a stage within a stage. Building a set of self-standing walls or dividers can be used as a portable backdrop. Your emphasis, then, is a smaller area which may allow more room for creativity. Risers can be used in front of the portable walls to provide different heights. A small choir on a large stage may look out of proportion. This same choir in front of a smaller created stage will be more focused and more confident. When creating a smaller stage, the children should not be crowded on the risers. Be sure that the stage you create allows enough room to do choreography. If the stage area is too small, individual children may be lost in a crowded group of faces.

Portable backdrops can be painted or covered easily with a variety of materials. They can be repainted and changed to fit a new musical every year. Canvas drawings can be hung on the dividers. These can be lowered like a curtain at a certain point in the musical to create a new scene.

This basic backdrop idea can be changed to four, six, or eighth smaller rectangular or other-shaped dividers. Both sides can be decorated. At a certain point in the musical, they can be turned around to make a new scene with a different look. If the dividers are self-standing, they can be moved to different positions during the musical, adding some variety. If you want to perform the musical at a local mall or the local park, your backdrops are ready to go with you. They could also be hung from the ceiling. The versatility of the dividers can add much variety to your stage.

Simple Ideas to Brighten the Stage

We use simple insulation foam boards instead of wood for backdrops. These lightweight boards can be cut fairly easily with a utility knife, and they accept latex paints well (no aerosols). They can be hung easily on stage with wire.

Children are able to carry this board on or off stage without any problem. This is much safer than using heavier material. Foam insulation board is relatively inexpensive for a 4-by-6-foot sheet. You can find this at any building supply store.

Christmas lights are a fun and fairly inexpensive way to decorate or outline a stage. Plan to buy your lights the day after Christmas even though camp may be months away. Outlining your stage with inexpensive fabric that fits your theme is another simple way of adding color and framing your stage. We built 4-foot square wooden boxes (about 1-foot high) that can be stacked together to make small stage areas. They can be used in a variety of ways–sometimes to spotlight a soloist. Or, a scene can be played from these small stage areas. We also built a set of six wooden boxes, various sizes and heights, for the children to use and stand on during the performance. The boxes can easily be carried on and off stage to add more variety.

One Step at a Time

Building a stage or adding to an existing one can be expensive. We are fortunate to have several builders in the church who donate their time. Making one major purchase a year may be all your budget will allow. Establish priorities. How do you eat an elephant? "One bite at a time." How do you build a children's music

SURVIVAL TIP

Emphasize the children, their faces, and their smiles. Spread them out and give them room to enjoy the music.

camp with so many needs? "One step at a time!"

Not every child can have a lead, but as directors, it must be our goal that they should all be seen. Determine if you need to build more distinct levels for children to stand. In our church's choir loft, we built a removable choir row to fit all around the upper row of the loft. You may choose to use a combination of your basic choir loft and risers. If you do not own risers, don't panic. Many times you can borrow them from a school or another church.

Risers can be set up in a traditional choir formation or used in a variety of ways to make your stage have different levels and personality. Two risers back-to-back, risers turned in different directions, or risers at different levels can create unique effects. Risers can also be used on the sides to extend the stage.

There are many large churches that have wonderful and extensive staging and scenery. But in a smaller church, the elaborate may not be possible. Frankly, the elaborate is not always necessary. Don't let the stage scare you. Don't be afraid to go simple.

Emphasize the children, their faces, and their smiles. Spread them out and give them room to enjoy the music. That is really what the parents want to see, and it is what we should emphasize. Parents want to be able to see their child sing, move, and interact. It is the Musical Director's job to work the stage so that the little girl on the back row feels she has a special place where she can easily be seen. She needs to feel that she is just as important as the child who has the lead part on the front row.

AUDITIONS

Auditions

The initial mailing of the Registration Form should include an Audition Information Form. (See Form PS-1 in Appendix A.) This will inform the families of audition dates and times. These auditions should be scheduled four weeks before music camp begins. The Registration Director, Camp Secretary, or church secretary needs to have a schedule in hand with any special instructions when parents call to arrange times. I allow 10 minutes for each audition. Remember to schedule a break for the Musical Director and judges if there is a long session of tryouts.

We usually choose two consecutive days to hold auditions. If a child is unable to attend either of those dates, I will schedule a convenient time for both of us. If it is not possible to schedule a mutual time, I do ask that the parents give me a video of the child speaking and singing. Please make sure the parents understand you cannot look at an entire video. They must have it cued and ready for you to watch only the child singing/speaking. I do this for my protection. If I give a child a part that he did not specifically audition for, over a child who made the effort to audition in person, it may seem unfair. The video becomes the official audition. I try to give every child that tries out some type of part, if possible. It may take several years to build up the number of children who audition. We went from 20 auditions one year to 50 the next.

I suggest videotaping the auditions. If there is ever any question about your decision or you need to review a certain child's audition, you will be prepared. this process may be more crucial if you audition a large number of campers.

The Musical Director needs to decide if she will need help judging auditions, or if she will handle them alone. Personally, the more judges, the more opinions and confusion. However, there is also a lot of pressure on one person when it comes to casting decisions. If you choose to have judges, consider using people outside of the music camp staff. You do not want some of your staff saying, later, "Well, I really thought we should have used X for the main part." This protects the spirit of your camp. If you use a team of judges, make sure they understand what you are looking for in those that audition. The Musical Director, ultimately, has to make all final casting decisions.

Desirable Characteristics

One of the qualities of a good Musical Director is the ability to see what other people cannot. This is especially evident in an audition situation. As I look at each child, it is not only talent that is considered. Some of the more important things to look for are the following:
• attitude
• a willing heart
• the ability to listen and do what is asked
• a happy disposition
• an eagerness to please
• a strong voice versus a weak voice
• the ability to project, or make the voice louder
• the ability to show emotion
• bright eyes, a happy countenance
• confidence

"Red Flags"
• the "I'm bored" attitude
• rolling the eyes, or crossing the arms, as if they really would prefer not to be there
• A child expresses that she cannot do something I ask, or does not want to do something asked. If this happens, I smile and go on, but put a big question mark by that name.
• giggling or acting silly
• difficult time making eye contact
• timidity
• the "I'm cool" attitude
• the hair is always in the face
• chewing gum during the audition

Audition Forms
Two forms (PS-5 and PS-6) are provided for your use in Appendix A. The next paragraphs describe Form PS-6, the audition sheet that I use. I grade in two areas: singing and speaking. The grading symbols are as follows:
• *Star*—This is an exceptional child. I give very few stars.
• *Check Plus*—The child did a fine job and shows talent.
• *Check Mark*—Child is capable of doing a part.
• *Wavy Line*—pitch problems.
• *Sound Waves*—Child does not speak loudly.
• *Heart*—Child has courage to try out, has a willing heart. Consider this child for a part that does not involve solo singing or speaking, such as a crowd scene, holding or bringing in a prop, signing, etc.
• *"A"*—great attitude.
• *"?"*—has a questionable attitude. The child may be very talented, but there is a reason for concern.

On these audition sheets, simply circle the symbols that fit the child's audition. For example, if a child sang well but had a questionable attitude, I would circle *check plus* and also circle the *?* under the Singing heading. If the same child did not speak loud

enough to be heard, I would also circle the *sound waves* under Speaking. A child may not be able to sing or speak. If he has a great attitude, though, and would put all of his energy and enthusiasm into a part, I would circle the *A* for a great attitude. I would also circle the *Heart*. That would alert me that this child would be a perfect candidate for a group scene or a role that did not involve singing or speaking.

If these symbols confuse you, use another form or make up your own and emphasize the areas or qualities you want. Symbols are good because if someone does accidentally see the sheets, they may not understand them. Some Musical Directors like to judge on a scale of 1-10. If you have several children that have a *Check Plus*, you could put a small number beside each symbol to rate that group. Example : *Check Plus* (4) or *Check Plus* (9).

Advice
I never let anyone look at my judging sheets. I keep them until camp is over for my protection. For example, one day during camp, a father approached me wanting to know if his son would have a solo. At that moment, I was able to find my judging sheets and look at that child's audition. In the tryouts, I had given the child a *Heart* and an *A*. I had carefully chosen a non-singing/speaking part for

him. I had also made one comment on the audition sheet (Memory ABCs). I had written this down because the child had problems with memory. As a second or third grader, he could not get through the ABCs without getting flustered and forgetting. He did this in his solo and every other exercise he was asked to do. This does not mean he will never get a part. As he matures, he may be a real star. But it was wonderful to be able to respond to that parent, kindly and confidently, and give them something to work on for the next year's audition.

It is also important that you do not overrate the children. I love every camper that auditions. My heart is for them and I want them to do well. Sometimes as they sing, my heart cries out for this child who may have special needs, family problems, etc. Many times I will write a sentence prayer in the comment section just to help me remember to pray for one of these. Even though I care for each child, I cannot give them all the highest ratings. I might as well not have tryouts. Be very honest on that audition sheet, and it will reduce the final selection time.

This manual suggests that auditions are best done in the church auditorium without an audience. The audition information Sheet (Form PS-1 in Appendix A) explains that the preference is for parents not to be in the room. This is because I need to see how the child will respond to me and my directions. When parents are in the room, the child's allegiance is divided. Children want their parents' approval before they respond, or look to them for reactions to my requests. I need their undivided attention for those 10 minutes.

Moreover, parents can wait outside the auditorium and listen. If this offends a parent, we will make an exception. The same audition is performed, but I do not push for the child's attention. I ran into a situation where the tryout became the mother trying to get the child to respond to what I said. She would go back over my sentences and explain it further to her child. Then she would explain to me why the child would not do what I asked. Finally, I sat down and allowed the parent to finish the audition. I was very kind; but, being unable to work with the child without the parent interfering, I couldn't give her a special part. I try hard to encourage every child. I brag on the things they do well. I do not mention any negatives. Giving out awards or stickers for doing a great job is also a good idea.

If you want a child to read from a script, this audition is the place. You may prefer to tell the children in the information sheets that everyone will read a Scripture passage such as Matthew 5:1-6, or recite a poem sent in the mail-out, or even a dialog from the musical. This will give the campers an opportunity to read over the selection and practice with expression. If you have a child read from a script unrehearsed, you will definitely find your best readers, but they may not always be your best actors.

For example, I had a child who was a great reader and was given a special reading part. He was a gift from Heaven! The next year, I assumed that his acting ability was equal to his reading ability. I found that he was very reserved and hesitant when acting on stage; but. if we put him behind a book, he was a knockout!

I learn a great deal from year to year. If a child does not make it for an extra rehearsal or comes unprepared, I make a mental note of that. If I give a child a speaking part and the child does not learn it well, or they finish memorizing the last day of camp, I take note of that for the next year. If some do not give 100%, it may affect their opportunity for the next year.

One final thought about auditions. Change and variety are very important. The 10-Minute Tryout is a basic plan. From year to year, incorporate different ideas and different songs. Make your auditions interesting and fresh for the campers each year. Do something they

THE 10-MINUTE TRYOUT FOR SINGING AND SPEAKING

This audition regimen contains two parts: 1-4 and 5-8. Campers auditioning for possible singing roles must complete both sections. Those who only want a speaking role may begin with Step 3.

1 Every child should come prepared to sing a solo with an accompaniment track. If they do not have an accompaniment track, I have extra tapes available from previous musicals. They can come by the church and pick up a tape and take it home to practice. No piano solos are accepted because I need to hear how they follow the taped music. After they audition, they return the borrowed tape to me.

I used to allow campers to simply sing "Jesus Loves Me" with piano. But I learned that an individual solo with a taped accompaniment is completely different. Timing, hearing, and feeling are very important. I also realized that it was important for a child to put some preparation and effort into an audition.

2 Each child is also asked to sing several scales: C, D flat, D, etc. This helps me hear the vocal range and the sound on higher notes.

3 Ask everyone to quote the Pledge of Allegiance as loudly and enthusiastically as they can. Demonstrate a few lines to help them understand what is expected. You should listen for volume and voice clarity.

4 I may ask campers to recite "Old McDonald" or "Mary Had a Little Lamb." Add some motions with the words of these rhymes, usually big and dramatic. Children repeat, including motions.

Choose one or two Exercises from 5-8.

5 Ask campers to do 10 jumping jacks as enthusiastically as they can.

6 Sing an echo song with motions, asking them to repeat.

7 Ask children to walk down the aisle and pretend they have just won an Olympic medal. As the crowd cheers wildly, campers must wave and express feelings.

8 Request that they say the alphabet with emotions such as angry, excited, sneaky, sad, crying.

These activities may seem silly, but they have real purpose. Because of limited time to work with extra parts, I must choose children that can be told one time to do something, and they quickly and cheerfully respond. If coaxing is involved, precious time is wasted. Also, the child may still do it his or her own way and not mine. I had a friend who watched several children audition. The first three children did the audition but with resistance. The fourth child held nothing back and went beyond any expectations. After they all left, my friend remarked, "Boy, that little girl was the only one that really did what you said." She saw the difference immediately. You will too!

are not expecting. Children with creative flair will rise to the occasion.

CASTING

There are so many children wanting an opportunity to have a part. Casting must be covered with much prayer. Ask God for direction and wisdom as you make decisions at every level. As Proverbs 3:5-6 says, "Trust in the Lord with all your heart, and do not rely on your own understanding; think about Him in all your ways, and he will guide you on the right paths."

The Director's Manual, available with many musicals to help you prepare, often includes a casting sheet. There is also a Master Cast List (Form PS-7) in Appendix A of this book. The casting sheet is a very important tool. Cast the major leads first. Sometimes in the desire to have the strongest speaking parts, we choose the children that are good in both speaking and singing. This is understandable; however, the major leads do not always sing. If you are not careful, that will leave you with many solos needing to be filled with children who are not as strong vocally. Take this into consideration as you cast.

In addition, it is very important to know your musical well before you begin casting. Take an afternoon or evening and declare it as your time of

musical study. Listen to your musical one time through, taking notes and brainstorming. Allow your own creative ideas to have a chance to blossom. Use the Director's Manual, and watch the video, if available. In the auditions section, we suggested rating the children with symbols. Rate the speaking roles and solos in the musical with the same rating system. Sing the solos and listen to the speaking parts, rating each as you go. then at casting time, you connect a star solo (one that is more difficult) with a child given a star rating in the Singing category or a check solo (less difficult) with a less talented/secure singer.

Experience is talking here. I had rated my campers carefully. With confidence, I gave my star actor the lead and worked down the list. As I learned and worked with the musical more and more in the days to come, I realized there was another part that had less lines and was not a major, but it required more acting ability and demanded a natural sense of timing far above all the other parts. How important it is to recognize these things before you cast. If you get to know the musical before your auditions and casting, you will eliminate much pressure and have the knowledge needed to make the best decisions. If you are working with a team of judges, you will also be better prepared to substantiate final choices.

The Audition Response Forms (PS-3 and PS-4) should be mailed as soon as possible. On the Audition Acceptance Form PS-3, there is a place for the page number of the solo and/or speaking part. I include my phone number so campers can call if they have any questions. If a child is assigned a role, his response form asks parents to make appointments for private rehearsal times on the Saturday before camp begins. It may say on the form that we need 30 minutes of practice, or only 10 minutes, depending on the part. Also indicate that children need to have words and lines memorized by that time. If some cannot come on Saturday, I will meet with them on Friday or even on Sunday afternoon. I make sure they understand that if they do not attend this extra rehearsal, I may not have time to give them any individualized help during camp week.

Cast Rehearsals
The individualized rehearsals with the cast members are, in my opinion, one of the primary keys to a successful music camp. As stated earlier, these are usually held the Friday or Saturday before camp begins on Monday. Parents are usually very cooperative in making the effort to come to an extra rehearsal prior to camp. One reason is because I work with their children to help them feel confident and secure in their solos or parts.

If a child has a solo, work on the following:
- Listen to the music before the solo and decide when they should start to move toward the microphone. Allow plenty of time.
- Practice walking to the mike from different spots on the stage. You may not know at that time the exact place where everyone will be standing.
- Practice picking up the microphone and holding it correctly.
- Ask soloists to smile at the entire audience before beginning to sing.
- Practice singing with expression, eyes open wide, and communicating the message of the song. Remind soloists not to stay at the microphone until the song is completely over.
- Practice putting the microphone back in place before returning to their choir position.

Rehearse as many times as necessary, so that when the child leaves, his mother is smiling, he is confident, and you are pleased as well.

When dealing with children that have speaking parts, the procedure is similar. It is most helpful to have the basic staging set for that Saturday rehearsal. Work on the following:
- Explain where the child will stand and what is taking place on stage.
- Walk through the scenes, starting here, moving there during the dialogue.
- Discuss and use the actual microphone. If it is cordless or a headset, there will be more freedom to move around. If it is a basic microphone on a stand, children will need to stay close to it to be heard. If there is an omnidirectional mike, more interaction between characters is possible.
- Practice facing the audience when speaking. Actors must speak to the audience, not to one another on stage. Children need to realize that this is not television. If they turn their heads away from the microphone while speaking, the audience will miss those lines. In order to look at another person on stage, they need to finish the line before turning to look. When the speaking is continued, actors should turn back to the audience, keeping their voice in the microphone. This may feel funny, but the audience must hear the lines.
- Practice projecting the voice, speaking slowly and clearly. I tell my campers to talk slowly enough that it feels funny; then, it's probably just about right. Often, children are careful to speak slowly at first; however, as the week progresses, they begin to get faster. During the presentation, when everybody is nervous and excited, everyone tends to speak faster. Have a speed limit sign, or other visual, to remind them to slow down.

During the presentation, when everybody is nervous and excited, everyone tends to speak faster. Have a speed limit sign, or other visual, to remind them to slow down.

• Speakers should have a rise and fall in their voice pitches. A constant high-pitched voice is neither understandable nor pleasant. If they try to speak too low, they grumble. Teach children to use vocal contrasts according to the text. This variety will carry better and be more easily understood.

• Everyone must keep their heads up and not down toward the floor.

• Practice using expression and hand motions for words that need to emphasized. Children need to be shown when and when not to use their hands. A few simple hand movements to emphasize certain important words add so much.

• Practice changing direction instead of facing straight forward all of the time. This adds variety. I sometimes tell the children to speak to one row of chairs on the left side of the auditorium; then, at a certain point, turn and speak to a row on the right side. They must, however, still speak into the microphone.

It is amazing that after just one rehearsal, these children are so ready and confident on their first day of camp. My workers say, "Wow! They could do this tonight!" But the nice thing is, they have a whole week to practice and build their confidence.

Curtain Call
First, it is important to note that a curtain call is not always appropriate. If the pastor is preaching or giving a devotional after the presentation, it may be best to move right into the message and skip the curtain call. If the musical is presented on a Sunday morning during the worship service, a curtain call is probably inappropriate. On the other hand, at the end of a week of music camp on a Friday or Sunday night when the musical is the entire program, a grand curtain call makes for a wonderful finale.

Often, people believe that the curtain call must be short and sweet. Many children's musicals have an instrumental section for a short curtain call leading into a vocal finale. This works fine, but they are designed for short curtain calls that do not allow time to recognize every child that has had a significant part. The children can be arranged on stage so that there is no movement to center stage but the spot light acknowledges them for a quick bow. The curtain call we do is more a part of the presentation and we get more compliments on it than anything else.

To begin, make a list of everyone that has any type of special part from least important to most important. For example, prop assistants, group scenes, smaller speaking parts, dialogue group, scene soloists (may be divided into groups if a large number), primary characters, main character leads, entire cast takes a group bow, music camp staff (optional). The background music for the curtain call can be the music provided in the finale song. You may find you will need to repeat it several times or you may choose to use another favorite song of the musical with background voices omitted. To estimate the amount of music needed as background music, multiply the number of groups and individuals times 10 seconds. As you begin practicing, the time and music required may be twice as long because the children are still trying to remember and get it right. As you practice, it will all begin to click and the background music may need to be shortened in order for the timing to work out right.

Personally, it works best for me to pick up a microphone and introduce each special part of the curtain call myself. I call out only the stage names or groups, not personal names. Those are listed in the program. If you choose to use another person to do this, it is best for the children to practice with the announcer during the week.

Here are a few tips for directing a curtain call:

• When a child comes to take his bow, instruct him to watch for the director's signal to bring his hands up and out slightly above his head; hold for one or two seconds, and bring his arms down as he bows, and then back up to the starting position.

- If several children are bowing together, they should meet and immediately join hands. It is very important that they wait until the director signals to go up with their hands. When everyone is in position and the signal is given, together they raise their hands about head height and where their elbows are at 90-degree angles. Children on the ends are to act as if they are holding someone's hand. The children bow together and come back to the position where their hands are at 90-degree angles above their heads then quickly move back to their original position on stage.
- If a child stumbles on the way to take his bow, forgets to come at all, or falls in the process, make sure the sound technician is ready to cue a repeat or another song for the extra time needed.
- If your staff come onto the stage for their bow they will need to exit so as not to block the choir. Give them a designated position to sit in the front of the audience or a place to move to as soon as their bow is over.

Each musical is different and the curtain call is as well. Make these decisions early in the planning process so everything can be practiced enough to run smoothly. Never attempt a curtain call without thoroughly rehearsing it In addition to the start of the musical, the finale is what the audience remembers the most.

Opening Night

A Note for the Pastor

It is important that the visitors see and hear from the pastor. He may or may not be aware of the schedule for the service and the musical presentation. Be considerate, and give him a detailed order of the events. Highlight the items that you would like him to announce or direct. If he is to invite the families to the fellowship afterwards, and you want him to give certain directions, write those out for him to look over before the service begins. This will prevent you from looking unorganized and him from feeling uncomfortable in front of many visitors.

It is important to recognize, and make a public statement of gratitude to, your pastor for his vision and commitment to the ministry of music camp. Parents and visitors need to see and hear this as well. Without our pastor's support, we would not have a music camp. A nice time to do this is at the end of a presentation with a big cheer from the campers!

Your Attitude

You must breathe slowly, in through your nose and out through your mouth. Your blood pressure is up and your pulse is racing. This, too, shall pass, but it's not passing very quickly. You keep saying that this is just nervous energy but you are not convincing anyone, especially yourself. If another person asks you a question, you may scream! As you try to talk to the children, you realize that they are all too hyped to settle down. You analyze the situation and realize that you are as well! How many more minutes before we start the show? No need to fear these responses. They are normal. It's "Opening Night!"

Now please understand, I know that Opening Night is not a church music term. In using this expression, I am not suggesting that you have a three-week run of the musical. Opening Night may be your only night. It is just a term to describe the first presentation.

One year, I gave the pastor an order of service for the evening. It explained that the children would enter the auditorium first. Then, he would welcome everyone and lead them in prayer. The musical accompaniment track would be set and ready to immediately begin. Nervously, I walked into the auditorium and gave our pastor the signal to start the service. I walked over to my chair, took a seat, and waited for the music. In a moment, the pastor tapped me on my shoulder and said, "Jeanne, where are the children?" In disbelief, I looked back to see all the children waiting outside the auditorium for their absent-minded director to call them to the stage. How could I have forgotten the children? This was a tragedy! How should I react to this blunder? Well, truthfully, I took a deep breath, laughed at myself, signaled for the children, and marched on to Zion! The show must go on.

Additional Comments

While, it is true that Opening Night does present its challenges, one is never quite sure what is going to happen. You may ask yourself the question, "Am I quick enough to run interference and smooth out all the bumps?" Face it with a sense of humor even though you are very serious. Regardless of what happens, my motto remains, "It was all planned."

In spite of its reputation, Opening Night is usually the best performance, because it has the most energy and enthusiasm. The children are so excited about their parents seeing it for the first time. An audience can do amazing things, especially one that really applauds. Also, the children are more alert to all that is happening. I prefer any video be taken this night even with the occasional "creative" moments.

Moreover, if the Musical Director has prepared well, the evening should go well. If it doesn't go as planned, remain positive. Smile at the children and let them see your pride in their efforts. Encourage them

with your expressions. Have fun and it will be contagious, not only to the children, but to the audience as well. The audience will probably be unaware of mistakes; however, they will sense your attitude as will the children.

One day, as a young teacher, I gave a child a disapproving look concerning a musical activity that we were learning in class. This child was not being disobedient or a problem, he simply had trouble doing the activity. Of the many experiences that I have had as a teacher/director, this is the one that haunts me. If only I could go back and change that moment, I would encourage that child. Don't ever miss an opportunity to build up instead of tear down. Although it's important to have a great performance, it is the children who are most important! If a mistake happens, sure, correct it. The amount of correction, though, should be small compared to the amount of praise.

Alert your staff to start applause throughout the musical in case of a subdued crowd. The staff's energy can be contagious to the children as well as the audience. The entire camp has worked hard for this moment. Enjoy! Let it be a memory to last a lifetime. And whatever you do, don't forget to bring the children on stage!

SURVIVAL TIP

Don't ever miss an opportunity to build up instead of tear down.

chapter 6

FINAL DETAILS AND FOLLOW-THROUGH

Gratefulness is the character quality that the Director should emphasize.

The Attitude of Gratitude

One of the most important things that the Musical Director must do is write thank-you notes. By the time camp is over, the last song has been sung, the scenery is down, and the lost-and-found box is full, I am ready for a long vacation! However, we are not yet finished. A thank-you note should be sent to all church staff, camp staff, and those who helped in any way. People who brought in food for the staff retreat room, those who gave scholarships, special guests, people who donated materials, those who built scenery, etc. are all included.

I like to write notes of appreciation using special lines from the musical. These are mean-ingful to those who have been very involved in the week and know the content of the musical. I send this kind of note to all the music camp staff. I also hand write a personal note to my staff so they will know that this is not just another creative moment, but a true, heartfelt expression of my appreciation.

Our photographer is very gracious, and always sends more of the group camp pictures than we order. Often, I write a personal note on these and send some as thank-you notes for the special guests, those who gave scholarships, brought food, donated materials, etc. Gratefulness is the character quality that the Camp/Musical Director should emphasize. Gratefulness allows others to know the ways in which they have benefited another's life. Although time-consuming, writing notes of gratitude is effort well spent!

Outreach

After a wonderful week of being involved in the lives of many families, it would be a shame to "drop the ball" and not follow up with them. Of course, the most effective tool is a personal visit. Our registration forms ask if campers and parents are members of a church. It would only take a short visit to find out if they are in need of a church home or have any other special needs that can be met. If videos were made and ordered, hand deliver each and have a brief visit with the family at that time. Another suggestion is to have a staff person take an individual picture of each child during camp week. Call for an appointment with the family after camp, telling them that you have something special for their child. Most parents are very receptive when something nice is being done for their children. Giving the picture to the child, and reconnecting, will help start a positive conversation.

Toward the end of the summer, have an enrollment party for your children's choir and the new school year. Rent a skating rink or have a carnival at this time. Invite all the children that attended camp, enjoy the memories, and discuss the activities that are ahead. Introduce a new musical for the fall or a Christmas musical that will be worked on soon. Teach one song from the new musical during the enrollment event. Remember to invite the parents as well. If you get the parents excited, the children will come. Even if you don't have an enrollment event, be sure the children receive an invitation to join your choir, Sunday School, VBS, and other special programs at the church. For those moving up to the youth group, send them a special invitation to the youth choir or other such activities. See Form F-2 in appendix A for a sample follow-up letter.

Other Ideas

It is always nice to start a tradition. Choose one great song, and teach the campers that same song every year. One night at the close of the presentation, ask all of those who have been a part of music camp through the years to come to the stage and sing this camp song with that year's camp choir. You might even send a postcard to the alum campers, asking them to attend the performance and participate. Anything like this might get a young person and his family back into your church providing yet another opportunity to minister to them.

Another tradition could be a keepsake collection of each musical presented every year of music camp. It could be called a "Wall of Memories." With permission from the appropriate personnel, choose a nice size blank wall in your church, hopefully in a high traffic area for visibility. Include a color, group camp photo, a few individual pictures of your leads in costumes or a group choir shot that displays the scenic background. Arrange the pictures, along with a copy of the program and any other highlights you wish to include, and have them all creatively matted and framed professionally in one picture frame. Years later, this memory wall will be a special place of laughter, smiles, and happy memories for campers and parents. It is also a great advertisement for your program and keeps music camp visible all year long.

The photo certificate that we give each camper at the end of the week is an individual memory keepsake from music camp. As suggested previously in this manual, find a photographer to come and take a group picture of your camp during the week. We do this on Wednesday to ensure that the costumes and T-shirts are ready, as well as to allow time for the pictures to be processed and back for the performance on Sunday night. Be sure to take a copy of the certificate and show the photographer as an example. We pay approximately $1.00 per

certificate. Our photo/certificates are black and white. One year, we allowed the parents to order a colored photo. We had to charge extra, but still sold several.

Reminders

As you turn out the lights on your music camp year, let me repeat a few details:
- Return the things that were borrowed.
- Collect books and materials that need to be returned or stored.
- Store costumes and props as space allows.
- Clean up any mess and throw away items not needed
- Set up a "Lost and Found" box or area to collect unclaimed items, especially clothing.
- Collect any outstanding receipts and close out the financial report on the camp.

Your staff will be very tired at this point. Organize the clean-up as efficiently as you have the rest of the camp week. If not, you might be handling this alone. The sooner you tie up all loose ends, the quicker you can look back and enjoy the memories. Although, I have found that there is no time to sit around and bask in the memories, for there is usually another major church project right around the corner waiting for me. That, thank goodness, involves another manual!

Budget Planning Form

Budget Allotment: $_____

Item	Estimated Cost	Day 1	Day 2	Day 3	Day 4	Day 5	Total Expenditure

Expenditure Form

Item	Date	Budget Section	P. O. Number	Amount	(Income)

Dear Friends,

The Lakeside Baptist Church Music Ministry is planning our first children's music camp:

~SUMMER MUSIC CAMP~

We thought that your children/grandchildren, or friends with children in your church, might enjoy hearing about this ministry. The camp is open to all six-year-olds (those entering 1st grade) through children who have just completed 6th grade.

The dates for SUMMER MUSIC CAMP are July 17-23, 2000. The camp hours are 9:00 a.m. until 3:00 p.m. Monday through Thursday. On Friday, camp runs from 9:00 a.m.-12:00 p.m. There will be two performances of the camp musical:

7:00 p.m. Friday, July 21 at Lakeside Baptist Church
6:00 p.m. Sunday, July 23 at Lakeside Baptist Church

The children will learn an entire musical in one week! There will also be times of Bible study, Bible quizzes, special entertainment, fun activities, a carnival, and a week full of singing. Lunch will be provided Monday through Thursday. There will be no lunch on Friday due to the early dismissal time.

Camp registration is $25.00 per child. This provides your child with a camp T-shirt, a camp picture, a book with recording of the musical (one per family), and a fun-filled week of activities.

*Important! Please try to register as soon as possible.

Registration is limited to the first 100 children.

Each parent is asked to be responsible for providing simple costumes for the presentations:
—long, dark slacks or jeans
—camp T-shirt
—white socks and tennis shoes

This year's MUSIC CAMP promises to be a great time in the Lord. The First Baptist Church family extends a warm invitation to your church and community to join us in this special time of music ministry. Please share this information with your family and friends so that they can be a part of this exciting week. Mail registration forms to:

John Doe, Minister of Music
Church Name
Main Street
City, State   00000

Please call the church at (555) 555-5555 if we can help you with more information or registration.

Parents, in planning for this week, please note that every child who participates in camp is also expected to be at all presentations of the musical. The performances are the highlight of the week. Mark your calendars now and plan to attend!

Joyfully,
Camp Director

Enclosures: Registration Form, Audition Information Sheet

(church name)

Music Camp Registration Form

Child's Name _____ Age _____ Grade _____

Street Address _____

_____

State, Zip Code_____Phone(s) _____ _____

Parents' Names _____

Church you attend _____

Are you involved in a church children's choir?_____

Would you be interested in talking with someone about our church?_____

My payment in full of $_____is enclosed. Make checks payable to:_____

Child's T-shirt size: ___Medium Child   ___Large Child   ___Small Adult
       ___Medium Adult   ___Large Adult   ___X-Large Adult

If you are interested in ordering extra T-shirts for family members, please mark the sizes and include
$_____ for each extra shirt along with your registration check.
(cost)
    T-shirt size: ___Medium Child   ___Large Child   ___Small Adult
           ___Medium Adult   ___Large Adult   ___X-Large Adult
           ___XX-Large Adult   ___XXX-Large Adult

Medical concerns, special instructions, comments, or questions
_____

_____

Please copy this form to share with others.

Mail to:

♪♪♪♪♪ Enrollment Record ♪♪♪♪♪

Camp _____ Year _____

Name _____ Grade _____

Address _____ Zip _____

Phone (home, cell) _____ Birth Date _____

Mother's Name _____ Employer _____
                                        Phone _____

Father's Name _____ Employer _____
                                        Phone _____

Medical allergies or concerns _____

Sizes: _____
        (shirt)   (pants)   (dress)   (shoe)

Fees Paid _____   _____   _____   _____
          Amt. and date Amt. and date Amt. and date Amt. and date

♪♪♪♪♪♪♪♪♪♪♪♪♪♪♪

Camper Identification Card

Group ID

(logo or
group name)

Last Name _____ First Name _____

Street Address _____

City _____ State ____ Zip ____

Home Phone _____ Mother's Name _____ Father's Name _____

Camper's Birth Date _____ Mother's Phone (work, cell,etc.) _____ Father's phone (work, cell, etc) _____

Grade completed _____

Medical conditions, concerns, or other useful information

In case of emergency, please call _____
Name   Phone

Camper Identification Card

Group ID

(logo or
group name)

Last Name _____ First Name _____

Street Address _____

City _____ State ____ Zip ____

Home Phone _____ Mother's Name _____ Father's Name _____

Camper's Birthrate _____ Mother's Phone (work, cell,etc.) _____ Father's phone (work, cell, etc) _____

Grade completed _____

Medical conditions, concerns, or other useful information

In case of emergency, please call _____
Name   Phone

WELCOME to MUSIC CAMP!!

Hello _____ and Parents!

(camper)

Please sit down together and read this letter. We are so excited about your being a part of **Summer Week of Choir**. Here are some details you will want to remember:

1. **Camp begins** each day at 9:00 a.m. and ends at 3:00 p.m. Children should not arrive before 8:45 a.m., and should be picked up promptly at 3:00 p.m. On Friday, camp ends at 12:00 noon.
   To make drop off and pick up times more safe and efficient:
   - Registration tables will be set up every morning to receive your child.
   - To pick up your child, please park and enter the Main Entrance.
   - When you pick up your child, please realize that this is not a time for questions or visiting. For the safety of the children, please receive your child, clear the building, and walk together to the car.
   - If you have questions, we are available before 9:00 a.m., or call in the evenings at 555-5555.
   - If anyone other than parents will be picking up, please inform the staff.
2. **Do not bring** your songbook or recording to camp.
3. **Bring your lunch** each day, except Friday when camp is over at noon. Drinks will be provided every day. Parents, please pack an individual lunch for each camper. We are not able to refrigerate lunches, so please include a cold pack as needed.
4. **Parents will receive** a Daily Newsletter detailing the day's activities, supplying Bible quiz questions, and alerting you to important information.
5. **Each child has been placed** in a colored-coded group for the week. (Camper), you are a member of the _____. You should look for the table displaying your color during registration.
6. Please remember these <u>important</u> presentation dates for the musical:
   - Friday, July 21 at 7:00 p.m. in the church sanctuary
   - Sunday, July 23 at 6:00 p.m. in the church sanctuary
7. **Costume Alert!** We are asking that every child wear the following for the musical presentations:
   - a pair of long, dark slacks or jeans
   - white socks, and tennis shoes
   - the camp T-shirt

Keep listening to your recording and we will see you on Monday, July 17.

Joyfully,
Camp Staff

Enclosures: Student copy of musical and recording, Audition Response Sheet

Send-a-Kid-to-Camp

Music Camp is just around the corner, and all the exciting plans for this power-packed musical week are coming together. Each child will receive a T-shirt, a book and recording of the musical, a week of fun-filled activities, and much more.

Enrollment is only $_____, but we never want an enrollment fee to keep any child from participating. *Send a Kid to Camp* is a way you can help provide for a child to come to Music Camp. If you would be willing to give a scholarship and make an eternal investment in the life of a child, please fill out the form below and return it to the church office, Minister of Music, or Music Camp Director.

Please call_____ if you have questions or concerns.
God bless you for your generous gift and for making a difference in the life of a child.

- -

Scholarship Card

Scholarship Amount $_____   Number of children sponsored _____

Name_____ Phone_____

Address_____ City_____ State & Zip_____

Name(s) of child(ren) you wish to sponsor, if you wish to specify:

1._____   Phone_____

2._____   Phone_____

3._____   Phone_____

4._____   Phone_____

Please make checks payable to:

- -

DAILY SCHEDULE

	Monday	Tuesday	Wednesday	Thursday	Friday
8:00 a.m.					
8:30 a.m.					
9:00 a.m.					
9:30 a.m.					
10:00 a.m.					
10:30 a.m.					
11:00 a.m.					
11:30 a.m.					
12:00 p.m.					
12:30 p.m.					
1:00 p.m.					
1:30 p.m.					
2:00 p.m.					
2:30 p.m.					
3:00 p.m.					
3:30 p.m.					
4:00 p.m.					

Suggested Class/Activity Schedule

Class	M	Tu	W	Th	F
Staff Meeting/ Coffee and Donuts Time:					
Early Bird Games Time:					
Music Class Time:					
Music Class Time:					
Music Class Time:					
Music Class Time:					
Quiz, Activity, or Craft Time:					
Refreshments/Recreation Time:					
Stage Class Time:					
Mass Rehearsal Time:					
LUNCH Time:					
Music Class Time:					
Music Class Time:					
Quiz, Activity, or Craft Time:					
Mass Rehearsal Time:					
Snow Cones and Awards Time:					
Parents Pick-up Time:					
Staff child care closed Time:					

Class/Activity Schedule

Class	M	Tu	W	Th	F
Staff Meeting Time:					
Title: Time:					
Title: Time:					
Title: Time:					
Title: Time:					
Title: Time:					
Title: Time:					
Title: Time:					
Title: Time:					
Title: Time:					
Title: Time:					
Title: Time:					
Title: Time:					
Title: Time:					
Title: Time:					
Title: Time:					
Title: Time:					

FORM SC-3

MUSIC CAMP!

Recruiting Staff Worksheet

Camp Director _____

Groups
Blue Bobcats _____
Green Giraffes _____
Orange Orangutans _____
Purple Panthers _____
Red Rhinos _____
Yellow Yaks _____

Early Bird/
Opening Assembly Coordinator _____

Quiz Leaders _____
_____
_____
_____
_____

Musical Director _____
Accompanist _____
Prop and Stage Manager _____
Drama/Choreography
Coordinator _____

Music Teachers _____
_____
_____
_____

Child Care Coordinator _____

Childcare Workers _____
_____
_____
_____
_____

Registration/
Camp Secretary _____

Adult Leaders _____
_____
_____
_____

Activity/Craft Leaders _____
_____
_____
_____
_____

Youth Leaders _____

Recreation
Coordinator _____

Recreation Leaders _____
_____
_____
_____
_____

Kitchen Aides _____
_____
_____

Kitchen
Coordinator _____

Newsletter Editor _____
Finance Coordinator _____
Registration Director _____

Carnival Coordinator _____
Nurse _____
Janitor _____
Reception Coordinator _____

Advertising
Publicity _____

Talent Share and Volunteer Sign-Up Sheet

Successful music camps and musical presentations do not just happen. This kind of outreach ministry requires much help and the cooperative efforts of resourceful volunteers.

Please fill out the form and circle an area of interest, talent you would share, or any way in which you could be of assistance.

Name_____ Phone_____

Music Teacher	Recreation	Crafts	Bible Games	Props
Registration	Publicity	Nursery	Costumes	Usher
Sound and Lighting	Scenery/Art work	Kitchen	Prayer Support	
Decorating	Drama	Baking	Staging/Carpentry Needs	
Carnival	Clean-up crew	Choreography/Interpretive Movement		

Return this sheet as soon as possible to:

Reminders: Music camp dates and times are:

Presentations of the camp musical are:

- -

Talent Share and Volunteer Sign-Up Sheet

Successful music camps and musical presentations do not just happen. This kind of outreach ministry requires much help and the cooperative efforts of resourceful volunteers.

Please fill out the form and circle an area of interest, talent you would share, or any way in which you could be of assistance.

Name_____ Phone_____

Music Teacher	Recreation	Crafts	Bible Games	Props
Registration	Publicity	Nursery	Costumes	Usher
Sound and Lighting	Scenery/Art work	Kitchen	Prayer Support	
Decorating	Drama	Baking	Staging/Carpentry Needs	
Carnival	Clean-up crew	Choreography/Interpretive Movement		

Return this sheet as soon as possible to:

Reminders: Music camp dates and times are:

Presentations of the camp musical are:

To Those Interested in Auditioning for Special Parts or Solos

Auditions will be held on Monday, June 1, and Tuesday, June 2, from 6:00 to 8:00 p.m. at Murdale Baptist Church.

Please call 555-5000 and speak with our church secretary to <u>make an appointment</u> for your child.

Anyone who auditions for a solo will need to sing with a taped accompaniment or track. Those wanting a speaking part may perform a reading of their choice or recite lines directly from the camp musical. Memorization is not required.
Parents: During the audition, we will meet with your child approximately 10 minutes and ask that you please remain outside the room. This will provide opportunity to work with your child one-on-one without distractions.

For your child to be given a special part, he/she **must** be at all presentations. Parents and children will be asked to sign a commitment form, agreeing to be at the rehearsals as well as the performances listed below.

Camp musical presentation times are:

Friday: 7:00 p.m.	Sunday morning: 10:45 a.m.
Sunday: 7:00 p.m.	Sunday-July 4th picnic: 5:00 p.m.

If there are any questions, do not hesitate to call before the audition.

Joyfully,
Camp Musical Director

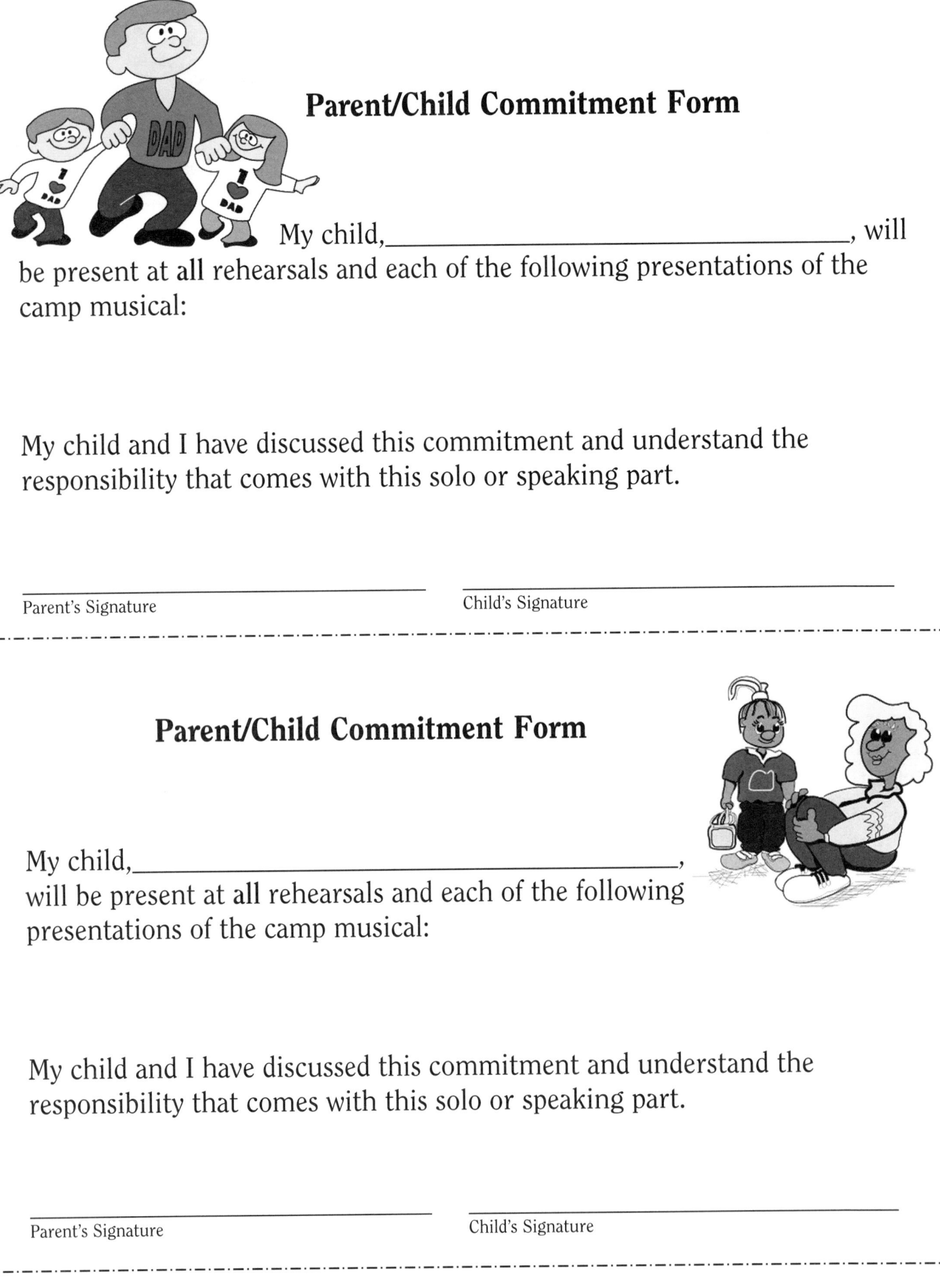

Parent/Child Commitment Form

My child,_____, will be present at **all** rehearsals and each of the following presentations of the camp musical:

My child and I have discussed this commitment and understand the responsibility that comes with this solo or speaking part.

_____   _____
Parent's Signature   Child's Signature

- -

Parent/Child Commitment Form

My child,_____, will be present at **all** rehearsals and each of the following presentations of the camp musical:

My child and I have discussed this commitment and understand the responsibility that comes with this solo or speaking part.

_____   _____
Parent's Signature   Child's Signature

Congratulations_____!

You have been chosen for the following:

☐ Solo "_____" on page _____

☐ Speaking part (character or page number) _____

Please learn your solo or speaking part, and then schedule a _____ minute appointment for a rehearsal time with me on _____ in the church _____. You can call the church office at # _____ to schedule an appointment.

Looking forward to seeing you!

Musical Director and/or Drama Coordinator

Congratulations_____!

You have been chosen for the following:

☐ Solo "_____" on page _____

☐ Speaking part (character or page number) _____

Please learn your solo or speaking part, and then schedule a _____ minute appointment for a rehearsal time with me on _____ in the church _____. You can call the church office at # _____ to schedule an appointment.

Looking forward to seeing you!

Musical Director and/or Drama Coordinator

Dear _____,

I am so <u>proud</u> of you for having the desire, courage, and determination to audition for a solo or speaking part in the camp musical. Unfortunately, I am not able to give you one of those parts this time. Please remember, though, how important everyone is who participates in the musical in any way. I'm so glad you're going to be with us, because this year's program is going to be so much fun for everybody!

You are a very special part of our camp and we look forward to seeing you next week!

See you soon,

Musical Director and/or Drama Coordinator

Dear _____,

I am so <u>proud</u> of you for having the desire, courage, and determination to audition for a solo or speaking part in the camp musical. Unfortunately, I am not able to give you one of those parts this time. Please remember, though, how important everyone is who participates in the musical in any way. I'm so glad you're going to be with us, because this year's program is going to be so much fun for everybody!

You are a very special part of our camp and we look forward to seeing you next week!

See you soon,

Musical Director and/or Drama Coordinator

Audition Rating Sheet

Name _____

Grade _____ Phone _____

Part Desired: ☐ Speaking   ☐ Singing   ☐ Movement   ☐ Non-Speaking

Speaking Audition (Rate 1-5)

Projection _____ Expression _____

Diction _____ Stage Presence _____

Notes: _____

_____

_____

Movement _____

Notes: _____

_____

_____

Singing Audition (Rate 1-5)

Pitch _____ Diction _____

Rhythm _____ Stage Presence _____

Notes: _____

_____

_____

Part Memorized _____

Attendance record _____

Behavior _____

Part in last production _____

Additional Comments

_____

_____

_____

_____

Audition Sheet

_____   _____   _____
Child's Name   Grade   Phone

Singing: Speaking:

★   ★

✔+   ✔+

✔   ✔

〰   ))))))

♥   ♥

A   A

?   ?

Comments:

_____

_____

_____

_____

Master Cast List

Speaking-only Roles

CHARACTER	ASSIGNED TO:	PHONE

Speaking and Singing Combination Roles

CHARACTER	ASSIGNED TO:	PHONE

Solos/Duets

SONG	ASSIGNED TO:	PHONE

Non-Speaking Roles

CHARACTER	ASSIGNED TO:	PHONE
_____	_____	_____
_____	_____	_____
_____	_____	_____
_____	_____	_____
_____	_____	_____
_____	_____	_____
_____	_____	_____

Special Choreography

PART	ASSIGNED TO:	PHONE
_____	_____	_____
_____	_____	_____
_____	_____	_____
_____	_____	_____
_____	_____	_____
_____	_____	_____
_____	_____	_____

Other

PART	ASSIGNED TO:	PHONE
_____	_____	_____
_____	_____	_____
_____	_____	_____
_____	_____	_____
_____	_____	_____
_____	_____	_____
_____	_____	_____

Rehearsal Planning Sheet

Date _____   Rehearsal # _____

Supplies Needed_____

_____

Warm-up Activities_____

_____

Minutes

_____   _____

_____   _____

_____   _____

_____   _____

_____   _____

_____   _____

_____   _____

_____   _____

_____   _____

_____   _____

_____   Total Time Planned

Post-Rehearsal
Activities_____

_____

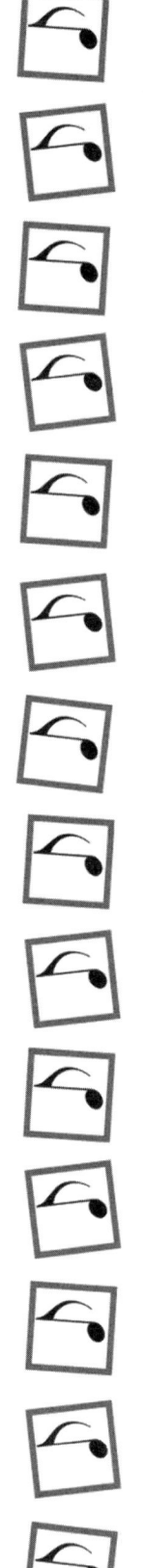

THIS CERTIFICATE AWARDED TO

FOR PARTICIPATION IN

SUMMER MUSIC CAMP

_____
date

_____
church

_____
Director

_____
Group Leader

_____
Pastor

Dear Camper,

It was a great week at Music Camp! We are already looking forward to next year when registration begins on _____. Over the next 2 weeks, we will have available a **"Lost and Found"** for any of you who might have lost something during the camp. The articles may be picked up in the church office anytime during the business day.

There are a lot of special ministries and upcoming events for kids your age. We have enclosed a list of some of them and hope you will be able to take advantage of these great opportunities. If you have any questions about the music programs, you may contact _____ by calling the church office at _____. The office will also be able to connect you with someone for questions about other activities and events as well.

Thank you for coming to music camp and don't forget the we want to see you again next year!!

Joyfully,
Camp Director

JUST A REMINDER

to _____
name

Please remember _____
_____
_____
_____
_____
leader

date due _____

JUST A REMINDER

to _____
name

Please remember _____
_____
_____
_____
_____
leader

date due _____

to _____
name

JUST A REMINDER

to please_____
_____
_____
_____
_____

need by _____

leader

to _____
name

JUST A REMINDER

to please_____
_____
_____
_____
_____

need by _____

leader

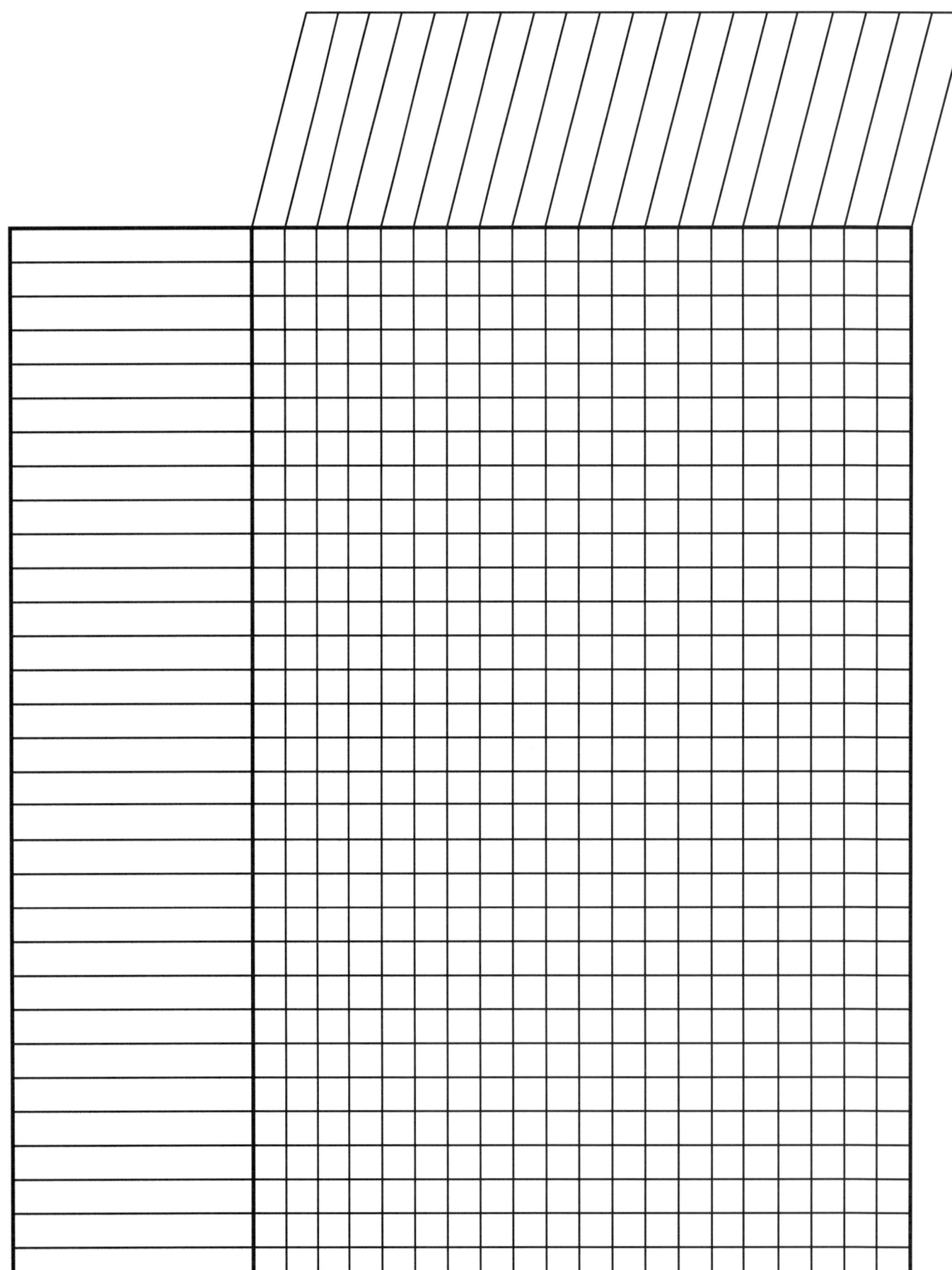

FORM X-3

MUSIC CAMP!

(space is provided for name of month)

Appendix A

FORM X-4

JUNE JULY August

BLUE BOBCATS

GREEN
GiRAFFES

ORANGE
ORANGUTANS

PURPLE PANDAS

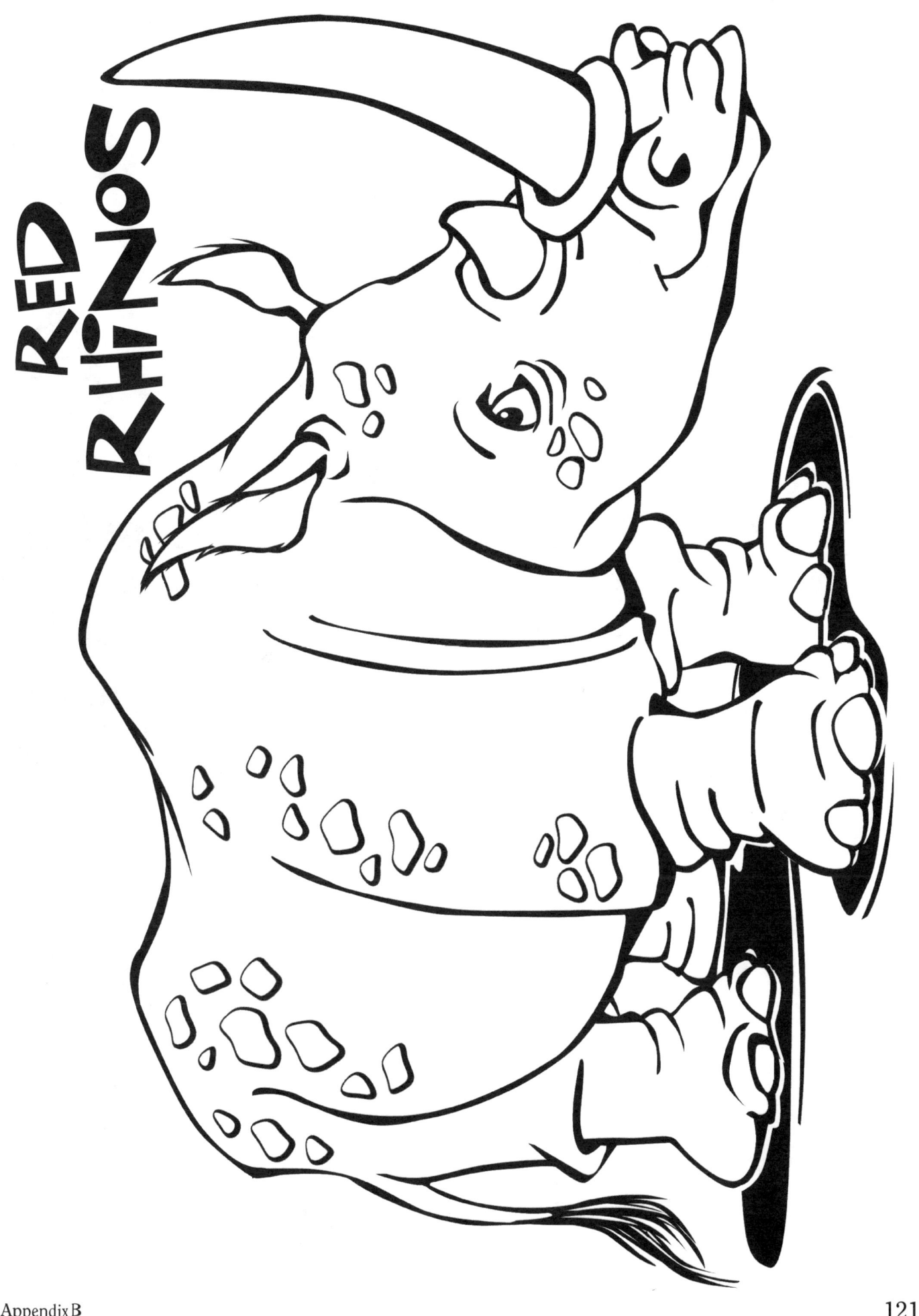

YELLOW YAKS

OTHER THEMATIC CLIP ART

The illustrations in this section are creative pieces provided to help generate other theme ideas should you decide to move from the animals and explore other fields of interest. Clip art for your use includes themes such as space exploration, building and construction, and creature praise.

These theme-related ideas were taken from different volumes of *Plans & Pluses,* the annual *Children's Music Series*™ resource book for children's choir leaders. See Appendix D for more information on this dated, yearly product.

name

name

Making Tracks

Watch _____ go!

You have really improved in

_____

Teacher's signature

SEE you at music camp
for a
Creation Praisin'
Sensation
time!

Praise Pass

name of camper

RAGING RAPIDS

MONSOON LAGOON

FOREST FALLS

WILDLIFE OASIS

CRITTER CANYON

RUGGED ROCKS

CREATURE
FEATURE

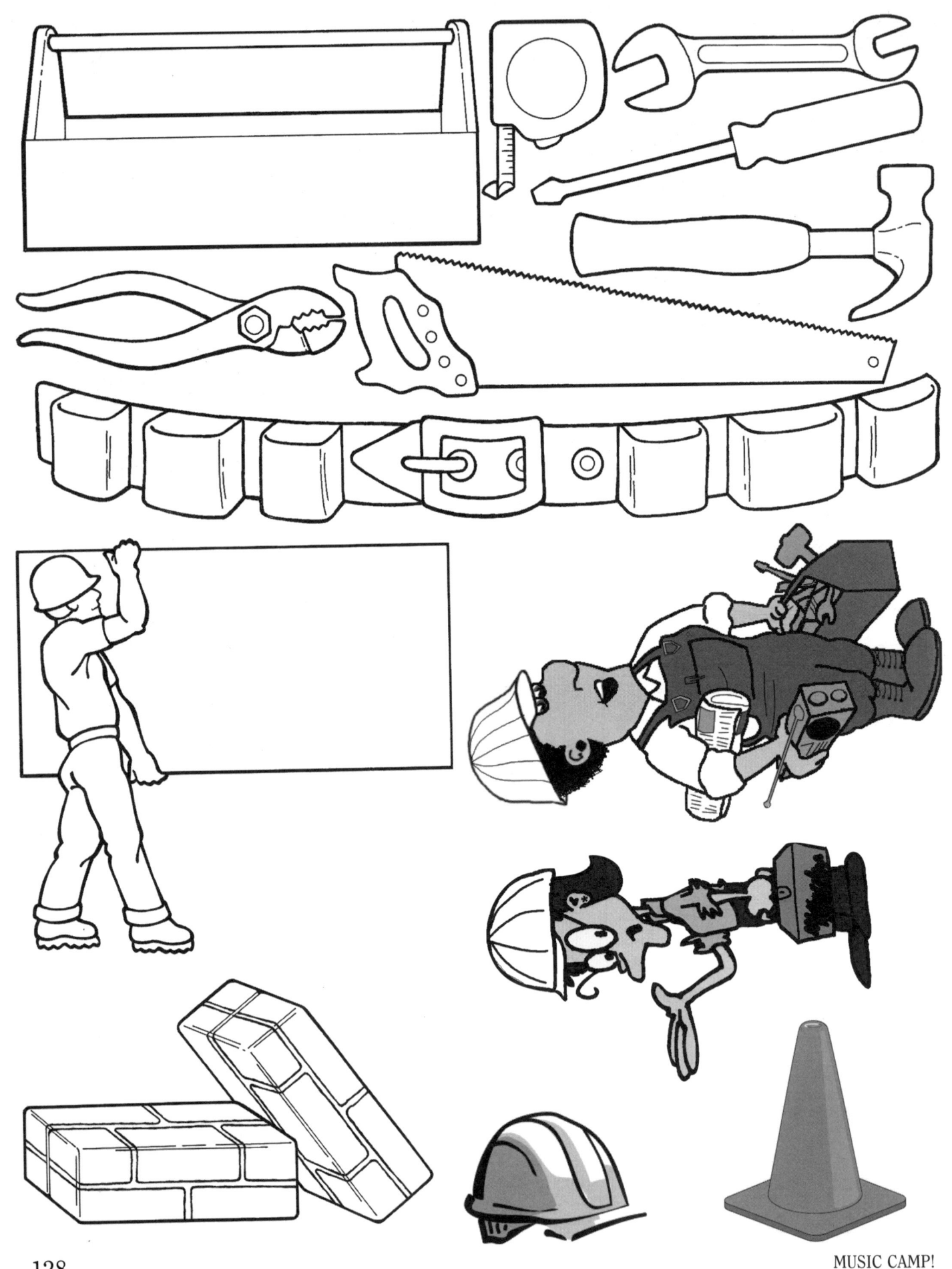

128

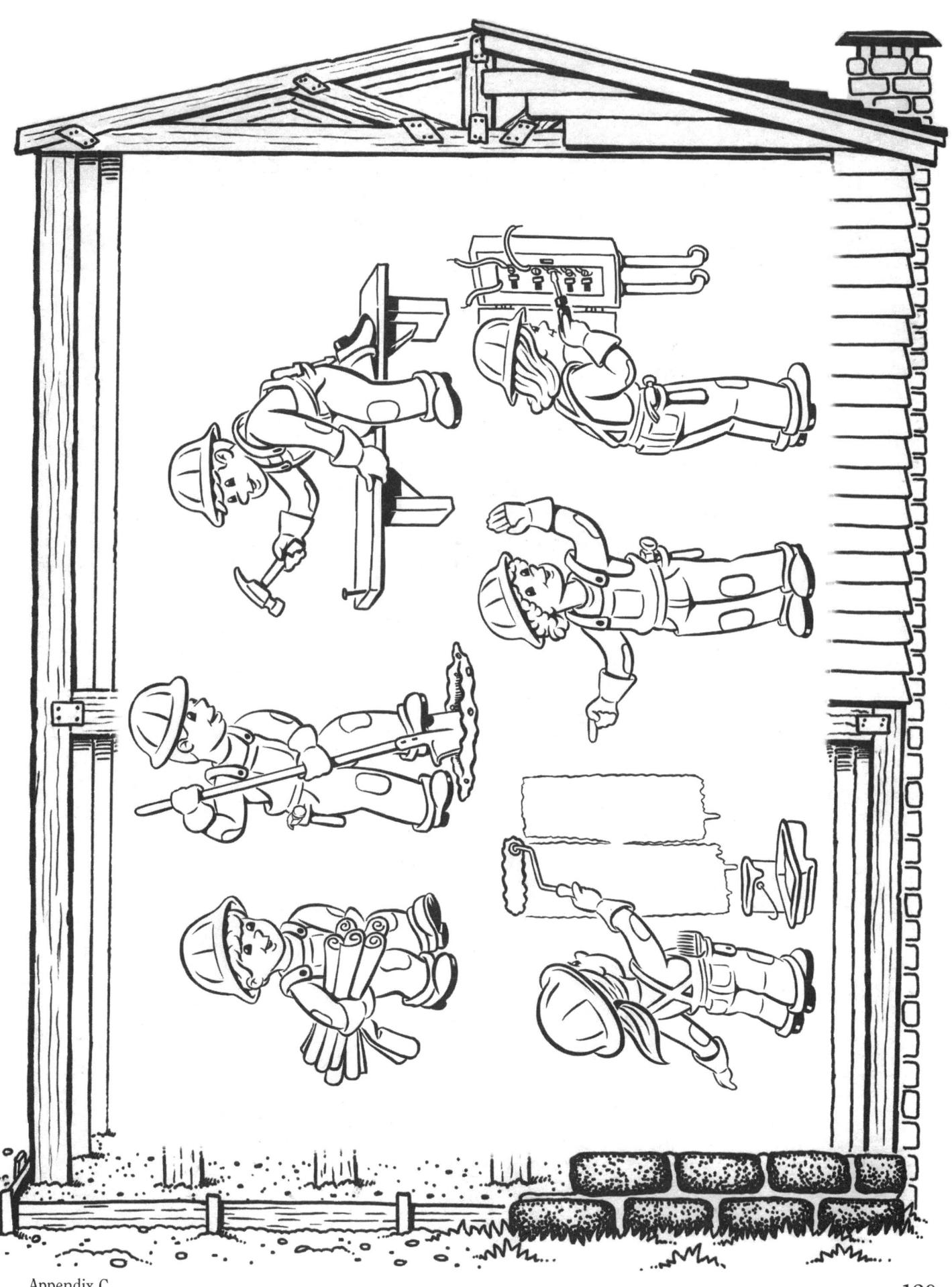

Choir Coordinator

**CONSTRUCTION
SUPERVISOR**

Choir Director

**CONSTRUCTION
CREW CHIEF**

Choir Member

**CONSTRUCTION
CREW
MEMBER**

for Choir secretary:
**CONSTRUCTION
RECORDER**

for Choir Accompanist:
**CONSTRUCTION
INSTRUMENTAL
CONTRACTOR**

**UNDER
CONSTRUCTION**

name

MISSION CONTROL
Director

name

FLIGHT
Commander

Mission Launch

Shuttle Ticket

name

Flight Crew

Music Camp
of

_____
name of church

begins

_____
date

at _____ **AM**

name

Discovery

Columbia
Apollo

Voyager
Adventure

PRE-FLIGHT MEAL

IN ORBIT

REENTRY

LIFTOFF
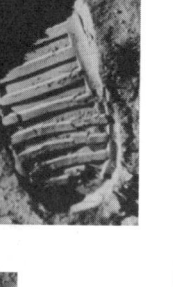

TOUCHDOWN

COUNTDOWN

Launch Pad
Space Station
(Registration)

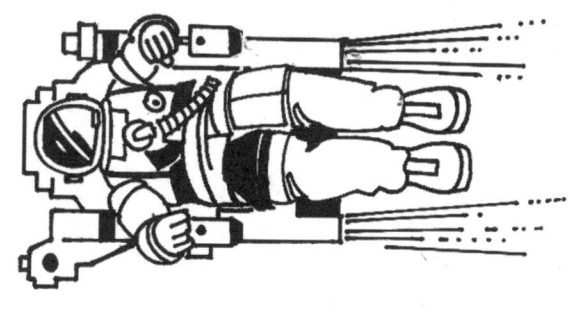

Space Center Mission Control

Make tracks to Music Camp on

date

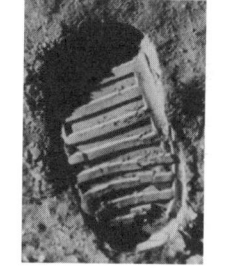

Endeavor
Enterprise

(Additional shuttle names to group crew assistants)

You're a
Super Camper!

LiFeWay Product Resources

The Good News Cruise
Jimmy Travis Getzen and Gail Getzen

Pull up the gangway, blow the horn, it's time to sail, so all aboard! Come join us on the *SS Good News* for a joyous, fun-filled cruise! In this delightful musical for children, events and activities on the voyage are used to explore, explain, and celebrate the abundant life found only in Jesus Christ. Titles include: *Celebrate Jesus; Soakin' Up the Son; Bible, Prayer and the Holy Spirit; This Boat Is Rockin';* and *For You Are God.* A promo pak can be purchased as well as listening and accompaniment CDs or cassettes. An instructional video and a Dovetailor (director's guide) are also available. DOVETAIL MUSIC

The Good News Christmas Cruise
Jimmy Travis Getzen and Gail Getzen

Spirits are high as the passengers and crew of the *SS Good News* prepare for a Christmas Eve celebration with the people of Laruba. The passengers are excited about a special gift they will present to the Laruba church: a beautiful mission bell that, for centuries, has called people to worship God. Titles include: *The Good News Christmas Cruise; Christmas Is All About Love; Abra, Abra, Abraham; Grand and Miraculous; Keep Watching, Keep Waiting;* and *Carol Medley (Silent Night, Holy Night/O Little Town of Bethlehem/The First Noel/O Come, All Ye Faithful).* A promo pak can be purchased as well as listening and accompaniment CDs or cassettes. An instructional video and a Dovetailor (director's guide) are also available. DOVETAIL MUSIC

Hallelujah! He Did It!
Pamela Clampitt Vandewalker

In this delightful minimusical for children, everyone can share in the joy and excitement of Jesus' resurrection. Using drama vignettes and amazing songs, this short but powerful presentation tells of Christ's miraculous resurrection, those who saw Him near the empty tomb, and of our call to share this glorious message with the world!

This musical is upbeat and energetic, easy to prepare and stage, and guaranteed to please everyone involved. Titles: *Beautiful Lamb; He Did It!; Have You Heard?; Sing Hallelujah!* A promo pak is available as well as listening and accompaniment CDs or cassettes. Bulletins and promotional posters can also be ordered. DOVETAIL MUSIC

Sticky Notes and Bible Quotes
Dennis and Nan Allen

What better way to guide children than to teach them God's Word? This collection contains Scripture songs and sketches relating to specific circumstances children face everyday. Got a sticky situation? Guide a child to godly answers found in His Word. Topics include fear, greed, self-worth temptation, forgiveness, and love. Provided on the enhanced listening CD are downloadable instruction sheets and cue sheets for a multimedia presentation. Just pop it into your computer! Also available are a promo pak, listening CDs or cassettes, and an accompaniment CD with split track. DOVETAIL MUSIC

Five Smooth Stones
(*Young Musicians,* Summer 2003)
Joseph and Pamela Martin

This minimusical is a modern day look at the story of David and Goliath. When crossing a stream at summer camp, children collect rocks to serve as reminders of the Bible story. They quickly realize that, while they don't face true giants in today's world, there are "Goliaths" in everyone's life.

The musical will be available in the *Young Musicians,* Summer 2003, *Children's Music Series* quarterly curriculum. The music/activity book contains 33 pages of songs and drama, plus a 24-page full-color pull-out section of related activities that teach musical and spiritual concepts. The resource pak includes reproducible lesson plan pages, an instructional video with choreography, a listening/accompaniment CD, and visual teaching aides. Titles include: *The Battle Is the Lord's; In the Valley of the Giants; God Is My Strength; Great Are the Works of the Lord;* and *Have Faith in God.*

The *Children's Music Series* quarterly curriculum for school-age children, Grades 1-3 *(Music Makers)* and Grades 4-6 *(Young Musicians)* provides a sound, core curriculum to help teach important spiritual and musical concepts. The age-appropriate activities provided each quarter would be a fantastic starting point, or supplement, to any music camp class lesson plan. *Young Musicians* fall curriculum usually contains a Christmas musical program and often provides a minimusical in the Spring or Summer quarter as well.

AmeriKids
Kathie Hill

Join the AmeriKids Convention in progress as Chairman Yacky Doodle, Rhode Island's Pip Squeak, and other delegates learn about the faith that made our country great. With words from key historical figures like George Washington, Ben Franklin, and Abraham Lincoln, this musical tells of the early 18th-century AmeriKids' faith in the Bible, prayer, God's protection, and salvation through Jesus Christ. Titles include: *Sing the States; One Seed, One Start; Build on the Word; Armed Forces Medley; America the Beautiful Medley;* and *In God We Trust*. A promo pak can be purchased as well as listening and accompaniment CDs or cassettes. A demonstration video and a Dovetailor (director's guide) are also available. **DOVETAIL MUSIC**

Hans Bronson's Gold Medal Mission
Kathie Hill

Olympic contender Hans Bronson is visiting Anytown, USA, to speak, but experiences a life-changing event instead. With help from three student reporters, he realizes his tremendous physical strength is no substitute for the spiritual strength of Jesus Christ. This musical presents the plan of salvation in a way that encourages kids to go the distance in their commitment to Christ. Titles include: *Olympic Fever, Hans Bronson; The Inside Story; The Colors of His Love; The Blueness Is Newness; Basic Four;* and *Better than Gold*. A promo pak can be purchased as well as listening and accompaniment CDs or cassettes. A Dovetailor (director's guide) is also available. **DOVETAIL MUSIC**

Truth Works!
Dennis and Nan Allen

Based on Josh McDowell's *Right from Wrong* resources for children, this best-selling, sports-themed musical is set against the backdrop of a school field-day competition. From the three-legged race to the egg toss, the students are faced with tough choices throughout the day. Along the way, however, they learn to make the best decisions. Titles include: *Do Right!, The Moment of Truth; You Are a Temple; Fair Play; Seventy Times Seven;* and *God Rules*. A promo pak can be purchased as well as listening and accompaniment CDs or cassettes. A Dovetailor (director's guide) is also available. In addition, the choral book and a demonstration/accompaniment cassette are available in Spanish. **DOVETAIL MUSIC**

The Plane Truth About Christmas
Jimmy Travis Getzen, Gail Getzen, and Barry Robertson

Stranded in Chicago's busy O'Hare Airport on Christmas Eve, one family decides to share the true meaning of Christmas with other travelers by putting on an impromptu pageant! Soon others are getting in the spirit, too. This fun, easy musical makes an ideal multi-age performance for grades 1-6. Titles include: *It's Christmas Time!; Nana Rap; No Fair! O'Hare, No Fair!; His Name Is Jesus; An Angel Came to Mary; Step by Step (Walking to Bethlehem); Hey, You! Keeper of the Ewes; What Makes a Wise Man Wise/O Come, All Ye Faithful*. A promo pak can be purchased as well as listening and accompaniment CDs or cassettes. A Dovetailor (director's guide) is also available. **DOVETAIL MUSIC**

Kings, Dreams, and Schemes

Jimmy Travis Getzen and Gail Getzen

Join an inquisitive bunch of kids and one curious adult as they pop their new CD in the computer for a "cyber" story about Daniel! As they click icons to witness Daniel's experiences with the king and victory in the lion's den, the stories are performed on the opposite side of the stage by others, while the choir sings of Daniel's awesome obedience to God! Titles include: *We Can't Eat the King's Choice Food; The King Had a Dream; You Can't Top the Power of God; The Handwriting's on the Wall; Three Times a Day; Dare to Be a Daniel*. A promo pak can be purchased as well as listening and accompaniment CDs or cassettes. An instructional video and a Dovetailor (director's guide) are also available. DOVETAIL MUSIC

The Dovetailor

Planning and producing a musical has never been easier! This comprehensive resource provides step-by-step instructions for everything you'll need to take you from the first rehearsal to the final curtain call—all within a 12-week period.

Here's what you'll find in each Dovetailor package: 1 choral book, 1 listening cassette or CD, teaching visuals, door and wall posters, a convenient three-ring binder with rehearsal plans, activities, puzzles, worksheets, detailed theme-related suggestions and more!

The following four collections are ideal resources for Early Bird or Opening/Closing Assembly gatherings, or any time needing a spontaneous song of fun or praise.

Cool Hymns for Kids

Don Marsh

This "hip" hymn collection, set in the style of some well-known artists, combines familiar favorites with contemporary sounds and rhythms in arrangements that will encourage praise to God that is timeless. Titles include: *Joyful, Joyful, We Adore Thee; Trust and Obey; 'Tis so Sweet to Trust in Jesus; Jesus Is All the World to Me,* and *All Creatures of Our God and King*. A promo pak is available as well as listening and accompaniment CDs or cassettes.

Cool Songs for Kids All Year

This contemporary compilation is overflowing with seasonal songs about special days throughout the entire church year. You will find dynamic selections arranged in an easy and fun style just for kids. Titles include: *Blessed (Thanksgiving); The Little Drummer Boy (Christmas); Thank You (Mother's Day/Father's Day); My Country, 'Tis of Thee (Patriotic);* and *People Get Ready (Commitment)*. A promo pak is available as well as listening and accompaniment CDs or cassettes.

Fun & Praise

This collection, compiled by Anita Wagoner, is filled with energy boosters and body movers for children of all ages. It has 20 timeless fun and action songs that will never go out of style. Just the thing for energetic kids, especially from grades 1 to 6, it's suitable for so many different settings. Titles include: *Wah-da-lee-a-cha; My Bonnie; An Austrian Went Yodeling; Singing Skills and Motor Skills; I'm Gonna Praise Him*. A Convenience Kit can be ordered that includes the songbook, a demonstration video, and a CD or cassette. Listening and accompaniment CDs or cassettes are also available.

Isn't That the Truth

These contemporary arrangements were created just for the purpose of teaching the truth about our awesome God. This wonderful collection of exciting Scripture memory songs is a powerful way for children to hide God's Word in their hearts. They will sing about the books of the Bible, the fruit of the Spirit, begin to understand salvation and grace, and have a joyous time praising the name of Jesus. Titles include: *The New Testament Song; No Other Name but Jesus; Salvation: Romans 3:23; Give Thanks to the Lord;* and *I Will Praise You*. A promo pak is available as well as listening and accompaniment CDs or cassettes.

This is a theme-based planbook that contains a CD-ROM and includes fresh, fun ideas for choir kick-offs, game nights, carnivals, or music camps. Plus, you will find helpful articles, promotional ideas, theme songs, and more than 125 pieces of clip art. Although this book is a companion for the *Children's Music Series* curriculum, it is a very valuable resource to have in your library.

For more information, a catalog, or to order any of these products, call toll-free 1-800-GENEVOX (436-3869), fax 1-615-251-3810, or email gmgdirect@lifeway.com.

Ask about joining the Dovetail Club of Inner Circle, a preview of the latest releases in children's music that arrives three times a year.

iNDEX

PRODUCTION STAFF

Dr. Terry Terry, *Editor-in-Chief*
Vickie E. Allen, *Editor-in-Chief*
Michelle M. Guy, *Contract Editor*
Tricia C. Watkins, *Contract Graphic Designer*

Music, Publishing, and Recording
of LIFEWAY CHURCH RESOURCES